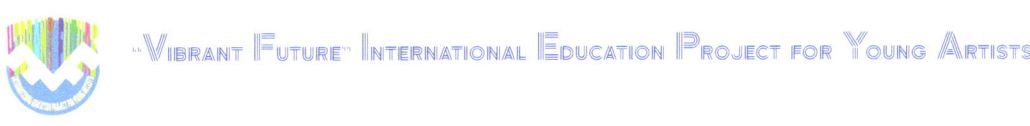

"VIBRANT FUTURE" INTERNATIONAL EDUCATION PROJECT FOR YOUNG ARTISTS

YOUTHFUL PALETTE

International Youth Artist Artwork Series-4

Artists: Elaine V. Kuang, Jiajun Deng, Ziyan Chen, Rong Hong, Lujia Gao, Junkai Gong, Ziqi Meng, Yihan Hu, Emma Chen
Editor-in-Chief: Mark Harris
Editors: Jia Zhong, Elaine V. Kuang, Jiajun Deng
Cover designer: Jia Zhong, Elaine V. Kuang
Book designer: Jia Zhong, Jiajun Deng

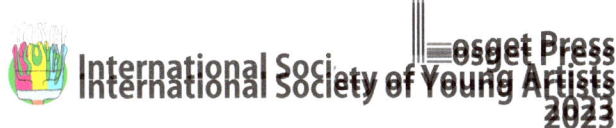

International Society of Young Artists
Eosget Press
2023

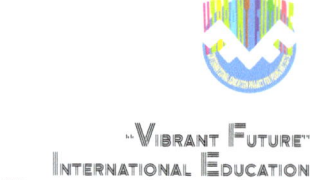

"Vibrant Future"
International Education
Project for Young Artists

Artists: Elaine V. Kuang, Jiajun Deng, Ziyan Chen, Rong Hong, Lujia Gao, Junkai Gong, Ziqi Meng, Yihan Hu, Emma Chen
Editor-in-Chief: Mark Harris
Editors: Jia Zhong, Elaine V. Kuang, Jiajun Deng
Cover designer: Jia Zhong, Elaine V. Kuang
Book designer: Jia Zhong, Jiajun Deng

 Copyright © 2023 by International Society of Young Artists
All rights reserved.

 Published in the United States by Losget Press, Los Angeles.
Originally published in paperback in the United States by Losget Press, in 2023.
Library of Congress Cataloging-in-Publication Data
Names: Kuang, Elaine V./ Deng, Jiajun/ Chen, Ziyan/ Gao, Lujia/ Gong, Junkai/ Meng, Ziqi/ Chen, Emma, authors.
Title: Youthful Palette: International Youth Artist Artwork Series-4/ Elaine V. Kuang, Jiajun Deng, Ziyan Chen, Lujia Gao, Junkai Gong, Ziqi Meng, Emma Chen.
Description: First edition. | Los Angeles: Losget Press, 2023.
Identifiers: LCCN: 2023902264/ ISBN: 978-1-951364-37-3
www.isoya.com
E-mail: isoya2018@gmail.com
First printing. 2023.

FOREWORD

The International Society of Young Artists (ISOYA) is a non-profit organization affiliated with Losget Academy. It was founded in Los Angeles in 2019 and has become a community of talented young artists who share a passion for creativity and self-expression.

In the same year, ISOYA launched the "Vibrant Future" International Education Project for Young Artists. This program is dedicated to providing exceptional artistic education to young people worldwide. To date, the project has inspired and guided 13 individual art portfolio books, as well as the stunning collective art book, "International Artist Artwork Series." This initiative has helped numerous ISOYA members gain admission to the world's top art schools and universities.

"Youthful Palette: International Youth Artist Artwork Series-4" is a breathtaking collection of visual pieces by nine talented teenage artists. These works capture the vivid hues and luminous radiance of their youthful spirits and offer a glimpse into their creative souls.

ISOYA extends an open invitation to all aspiring young artists and art enthusiasts to join our community. Our mission is to discover and nurture the artistic potential of young people by providing them with the tools and resources necessary to realize their dreams. As a non-profit organization, we deeply appreciate the generous support and contributions of the public.

May the seeds of artistic expression planted in every young artist bloom into a kaleidoscope of brilliant blossoms. Fueled by the fertile soil of education and nourished by the refreshing dew of inspiration, these budding talents will produce the sweetest nectar of art.

Mark Harris
President of the International Society of Young Artists
January 2023

The Liberty Awards

Awarded for outstanding achievements in the field of art by young American and international artists, the award is presented by the International Society of Young Artists. It was first awarded in 2018.

ENTRY REQUIREMENTS:
1. Entrants must be between the ages of 8-28 and from any country except those with which the U.S. government prohibits cultural exchange.
2. All forms of visual art are accepted, including painting, photography, sculpture, etc. However, any content deemed unsuitable for persons under the age of 18 will be rejected.

SUBMISSION OF ENTRIES:
Entrants are required to submit one or more images of their work via email, along with the work's title, the author's name, age, and country. Images must be in JPG or PNG format and between 1MB and 10MB in size. Upon receipt, an e-Certificate will be sent to the email address from which the message was sent. Entries can be submitted to the following email address: isoya2018@gmail.com.

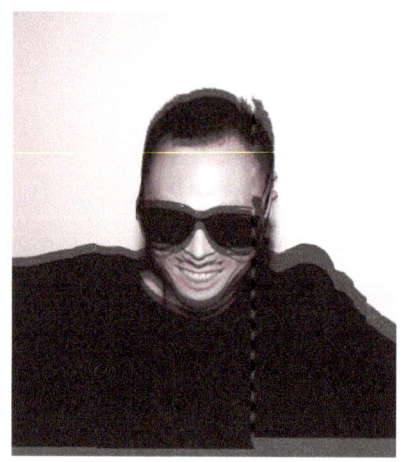

MARK HARRIS, Jury Chair
Artist/ Litterateur/ President of the International Society of Young Artists/ President of Losget Press
His 3 art books and 7 literary books have been published, and he has served as the editor-in-chief of more than 20 books. One of his philosophical works was included in Gaokao paper.
MAJOR ART BOOKS: Michelangelo's God Is an Alien Astronaut, East 100, Friar Hill, Illusion.
MAJOR LITERATURE BOOKS: Skeleton Garden, Michelangelo DiCaprio, Book of Chinese Homophones, Book of Chinese Full-Rhymes, Book of Chinese Alliterations.

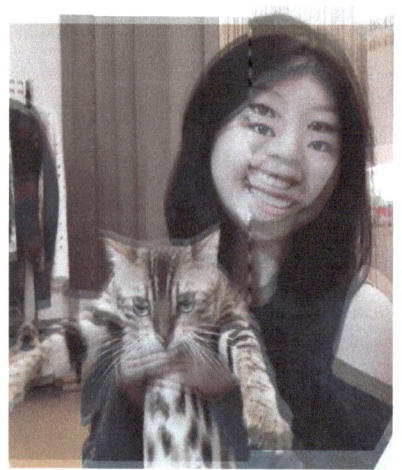

JIA ZHONG, Judge
She is a graduate of the Illustration Department at the School of Visual Art in New York. Her work takes a unique approach to the relationship between humankind and nature. Through a series of imaginative landscape paintings, she highlights the essential need for reverence toward nature. Her art captures the spirit of nature in a way that celebrates its beauty and power. As Shakespeare once said, "All the world's a stage," and she uses her art to showcase the magnificence of the natural world.

YAXIN TU, Judge

She is a graduate of the Illustration Department at the School of Visual Art in New York and is currently studying Art Business at Sotheby's Institute of Art. With a solid background in painting and early exposure to art, she has gained rich experience and a deep understanding of various sectors in the art world, coupled with an international perspective. Her expertise lies in printmaking, watercolor, and oil painting, but she is currently exploring digital art and aims to exhibit her work as a digital artist.

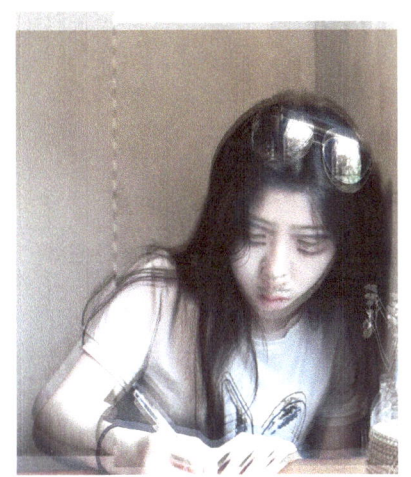

EMIRI FUJIMOTO, Judge

Born in Japan and raised in China, she currently resides and works in New York as an interdisciplinary artist, primarily focusing on sculpture and performance. Her practice centers around found objects and craft techniques. She obtained a BFA from the Visual and Critical Studies department at the School of Visual Arts, and her works have been exhibited at various venues, including the Wolf Building and O'Flaherty's in New York, as well as Tilly Foster Farm in Brewster, NY.

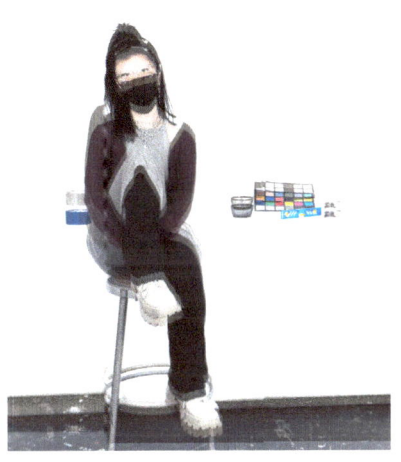

FANGNI WU, Judge

She is a graduate of the Illustration Department at the School of Visual Art in New York and has a distinctive style that features bright colors, intricate patterns, and attention to detail. In 2020, she participated in the Shanghai Children's Book Fair, where she showcased and sold her original illustrations. In 2021, she spent several months volunteering at Chengdu Luhu A4 Art Museum and Tianfu Art Park, which broadened her perspective and artistic experience. Fangni is currently based in Tokyo, where she continues to develop her skills in illustration.

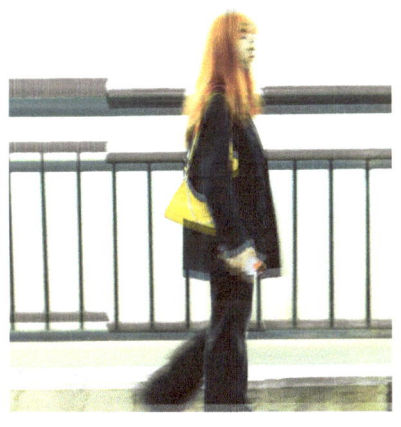

Contents

Elaine V. Kuang 2
Jiajun Deng 10
Ziyan Chen 18
Rong Hong 26
Lujia Gao 34
Junkai Gong 42
Ziqi Meng 48
Yihan Hu 56
Emma Chen 64
The "Vibrant Future" International Education Project for Young Artists Publications List 70
The Young Picture Book Artists Program Publications List 71
Publication Information 72

YOUTHFUL PALETTE
International Youth Artist Artwork Series-4

ELAINE V. KUANG
Ruben S. Ayala High School, USA

Schools that have accepted her for the 2023 Fall semester:
- School of the Art Institute of Chicago
- School of Visual Arts
- ArtCenter College of Design
- Pratt Institute
- PrattMWP College of Art and Design
- California College of the Arts
- University of California, Irvine
- University of California, San Diego

- Person of the Year 2022, International Society of Young Artists, USA, 2022.
- Gold Award for Art, 5th Liberty Awards, International Society of Young Artists, USA, 2022.
- Person of the Year 2021, International Society of Young Artists, USA, 2021.
- Gold Award for Art, 4th Liberty Awards, International Society of Young Artists, USA, 2021.
- Gold Award for Art, 3rd Liberty Awards, International Society of Young Artists, USA, 2020.
- Person of the Year 2019, International Society of Young Artists, USA, 2019.
- Gold Award for Art, 2nd Liberty Awards, International Society of Young Artists, USA, 2019.
- Bronze Award for Art, 1st Liberty Awards, International Society of Young Artists, USA, 2018.

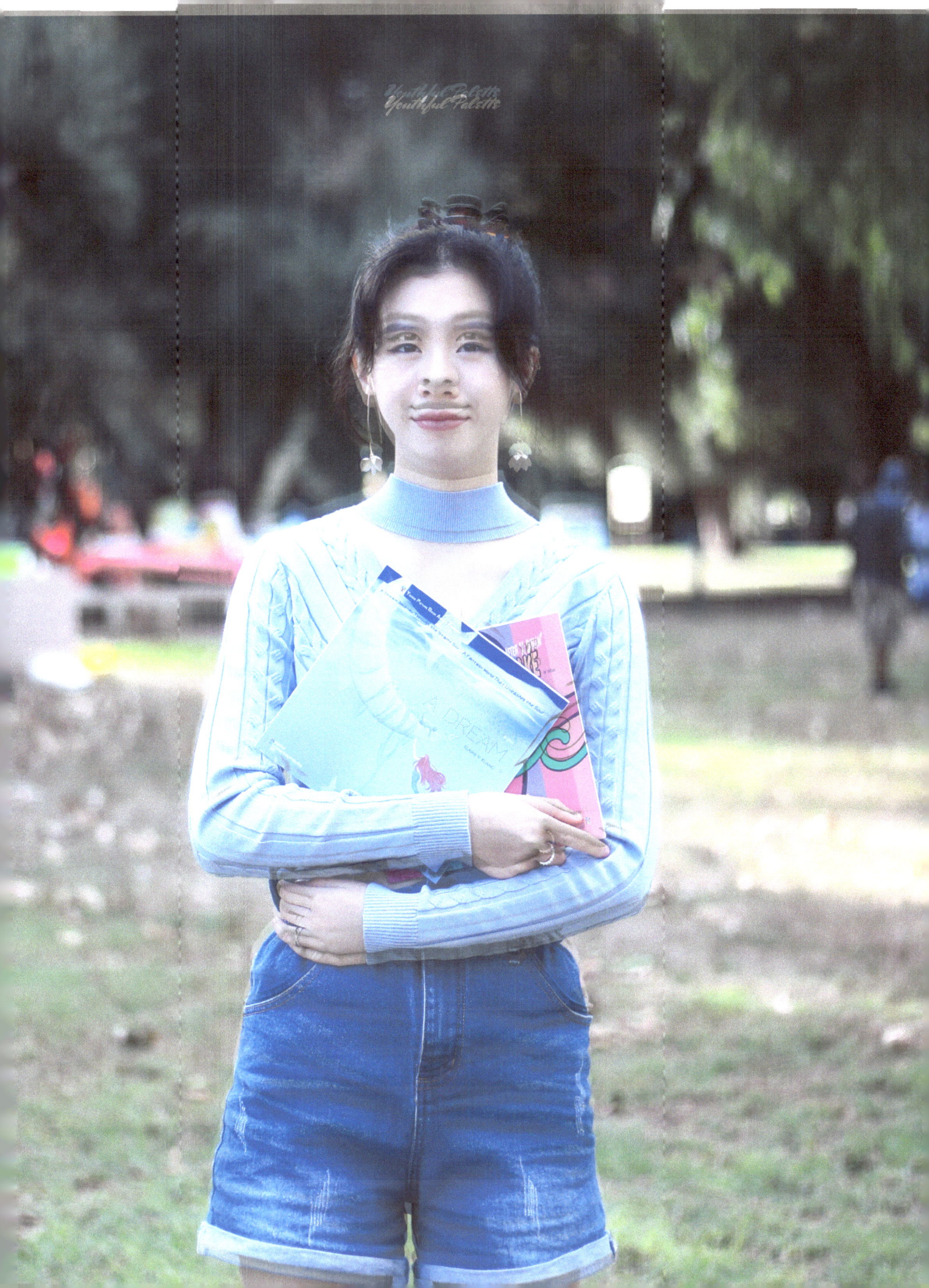

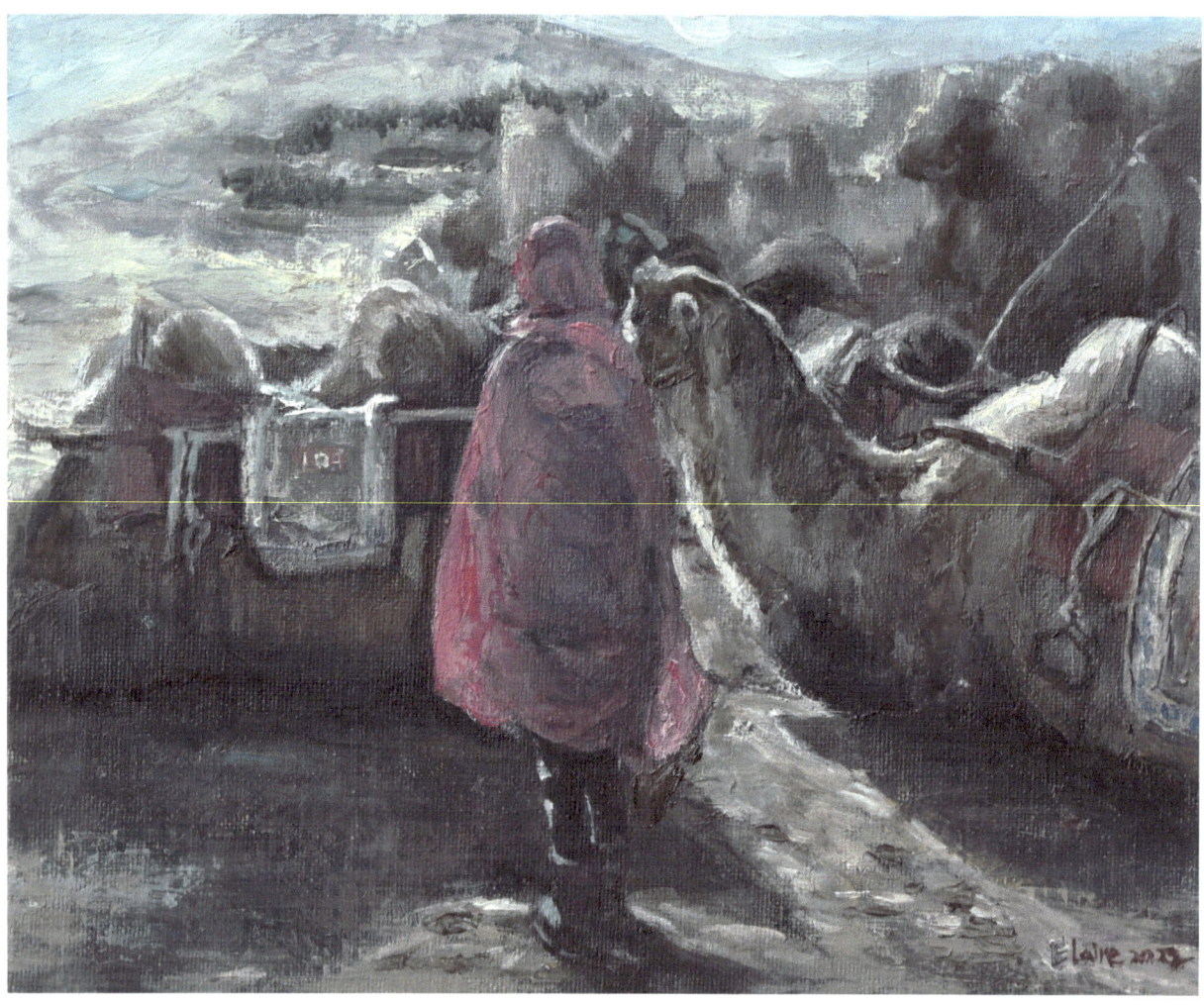

Girl and Camels, oil on canvas, 2022.

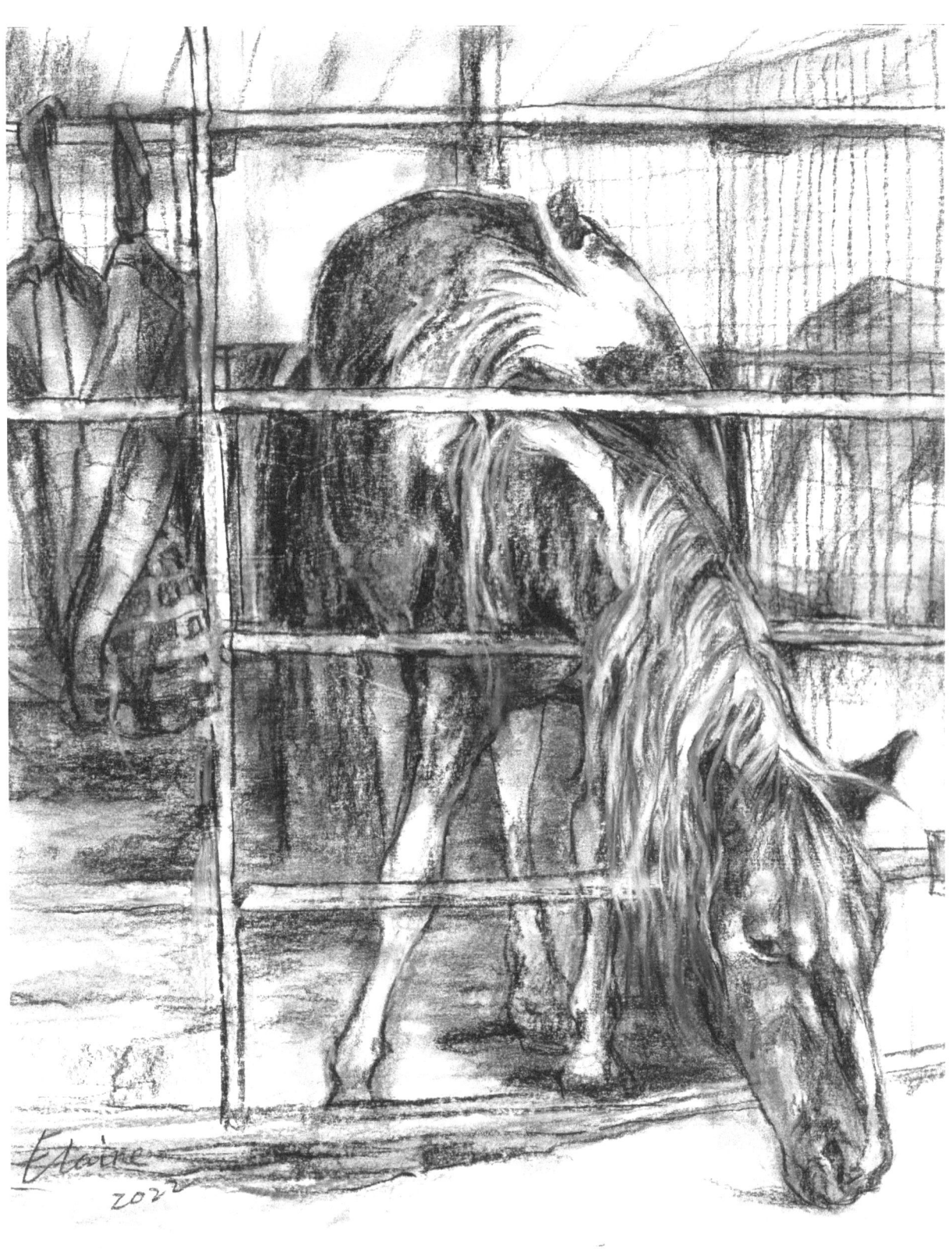

Imprisoned Horses, oil on canvas, 2022.

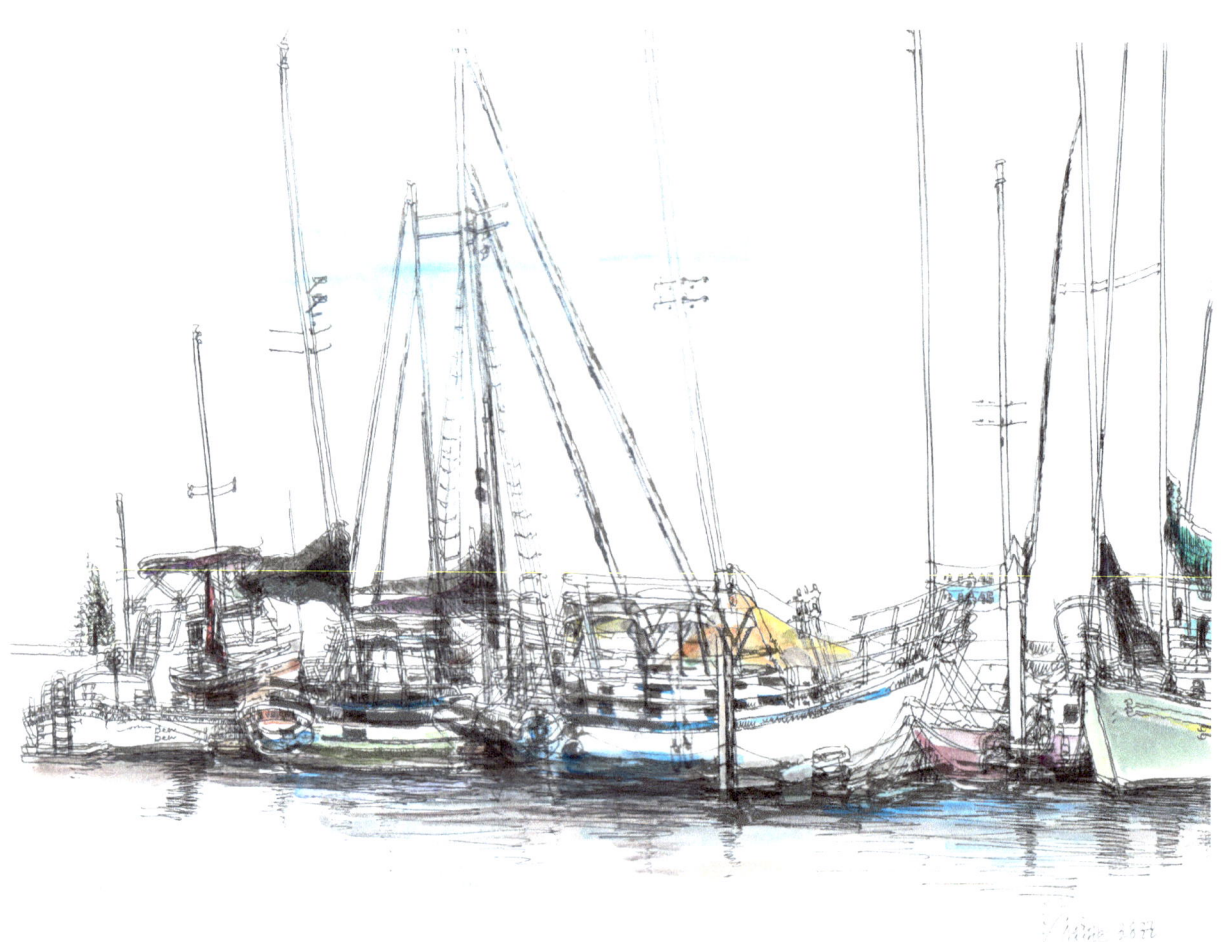

Yachts at Key West, pen and acrylic on paper, 2022.

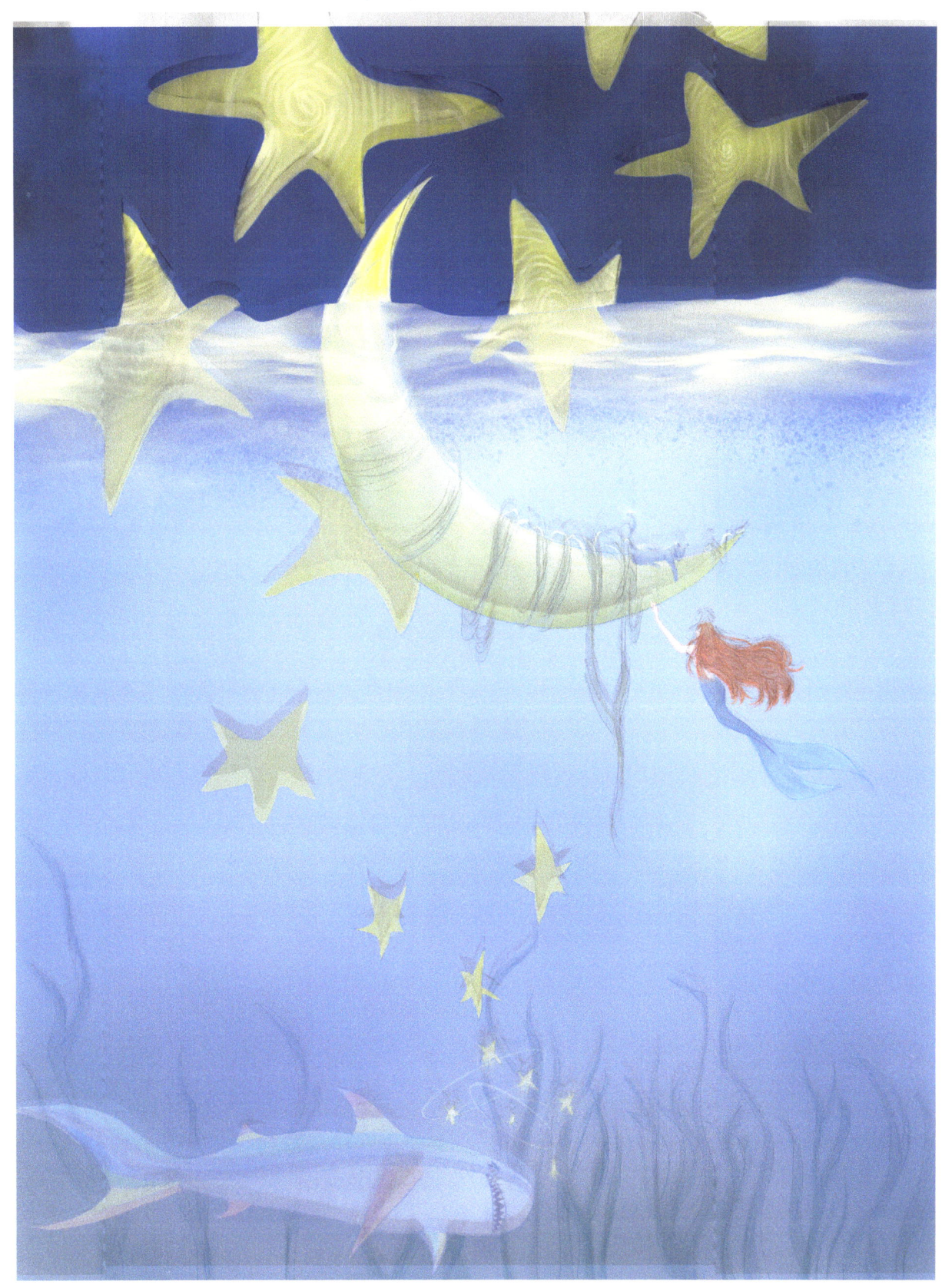

Page Selection in Picture Book *A Dream*, digital, 2022.

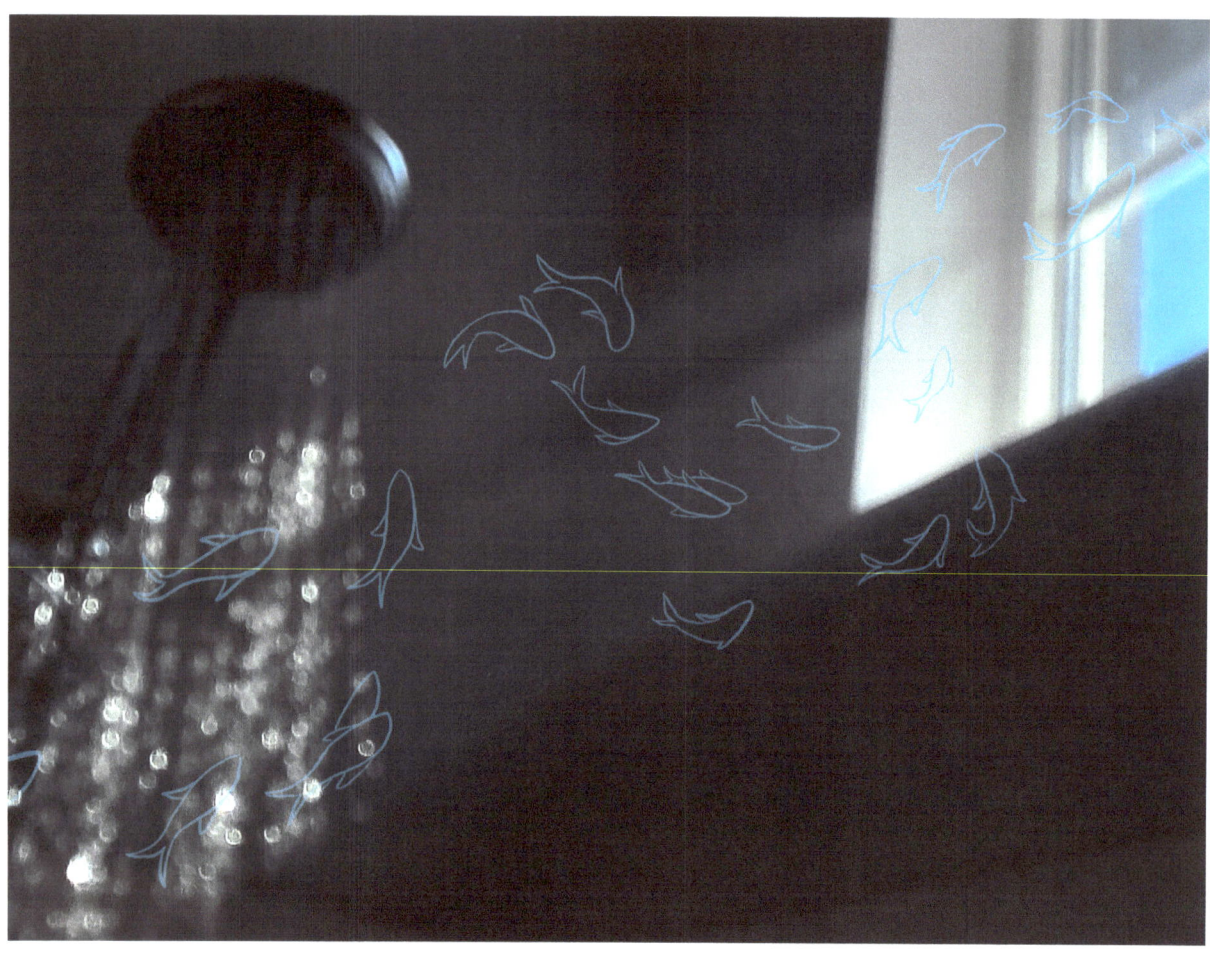

Across the River to the Sky, photography and digital, 2022.

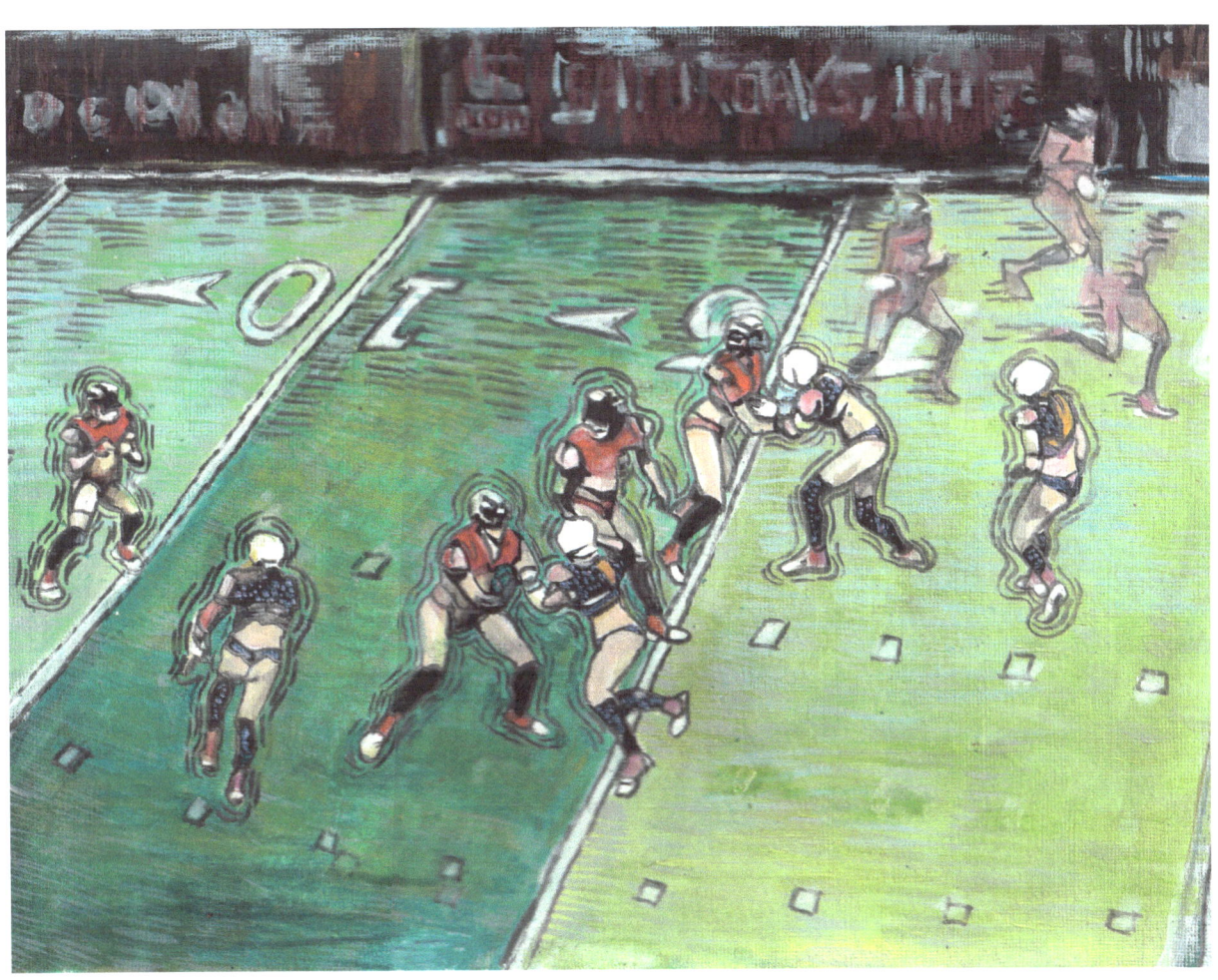

Women's American Football, pencil, oil pastel, and acrylic on paper, 2022.

JIAJUN DENG
Qingdao No.17 High School, China

Schools that have accepted her for the 2023 Fall semester:
- Rhode Island School of Design (WL)
- School of the Art Institute of Chicago
- Parsons School of Design | The New School
- School of Visual Arts
- Pratt Institute
- California College of the Arts
- Savannah College of Arts and Design

- Gold Award for Art, 5th Liberty Awards, International Society of Young Artists, USA, 2022.
- Gold Award for Art, 4th Liberty Awards, International Society of Young Artists, USA, 2021.
- Person of the Year 2020, International Society of Young Artists, USA, 2020.
- Gold Award for Art, 3rd Liberty Awards, International Society of Young Artists, USA, 2020.
- Silver Award for Art, 2nd Liberty Awards, International Society of Young Artists, USA, 2019.
- Gold Award for Art, 1st Liberty Awards, International Society of Young Artists, USA, 2018.
- Gold Award, "The Colorful Peace" Art Project Honoring the 100th Anniversary of the WWI Armistice, International Society of Young Artists, USA, 2018.

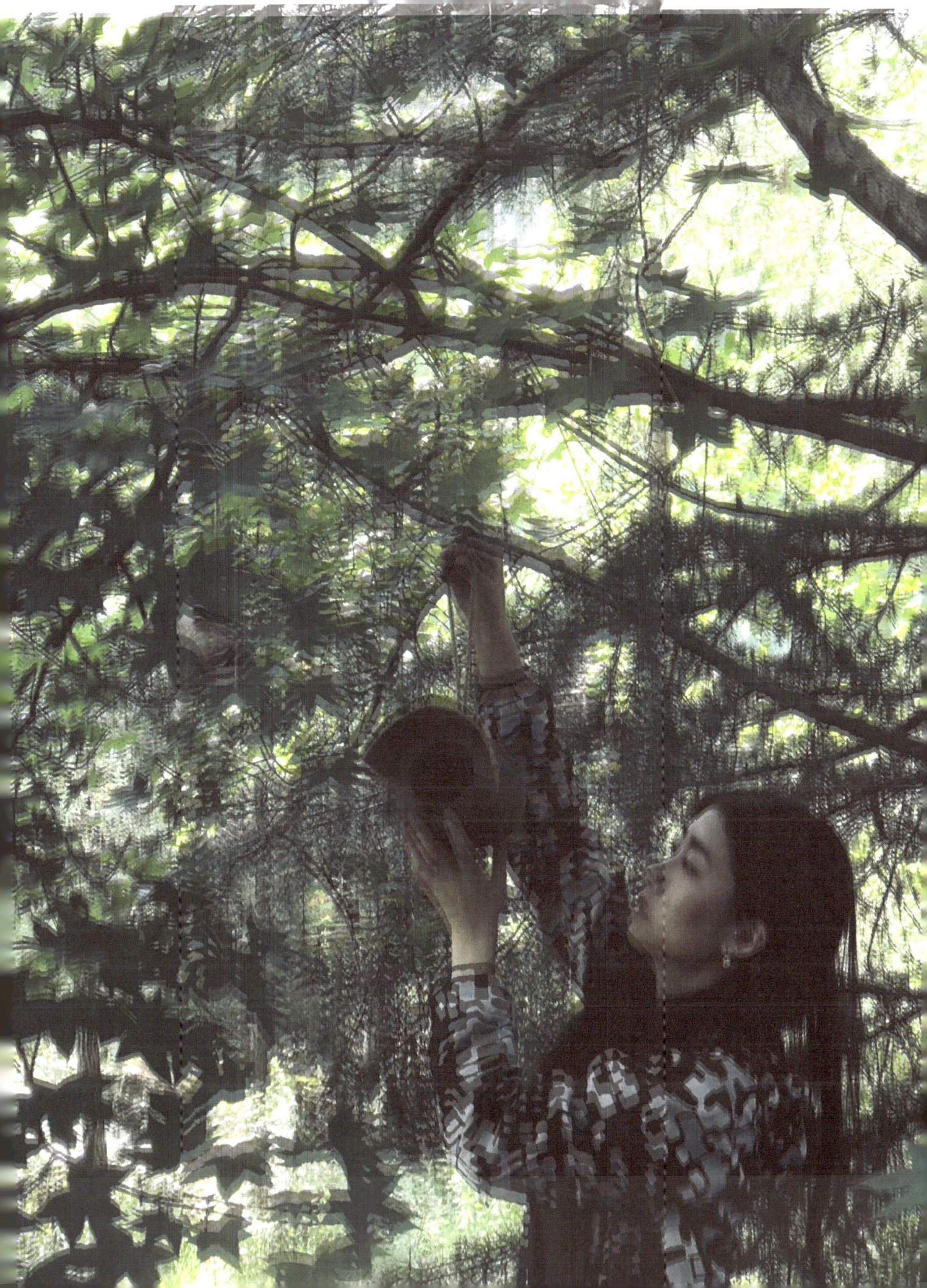

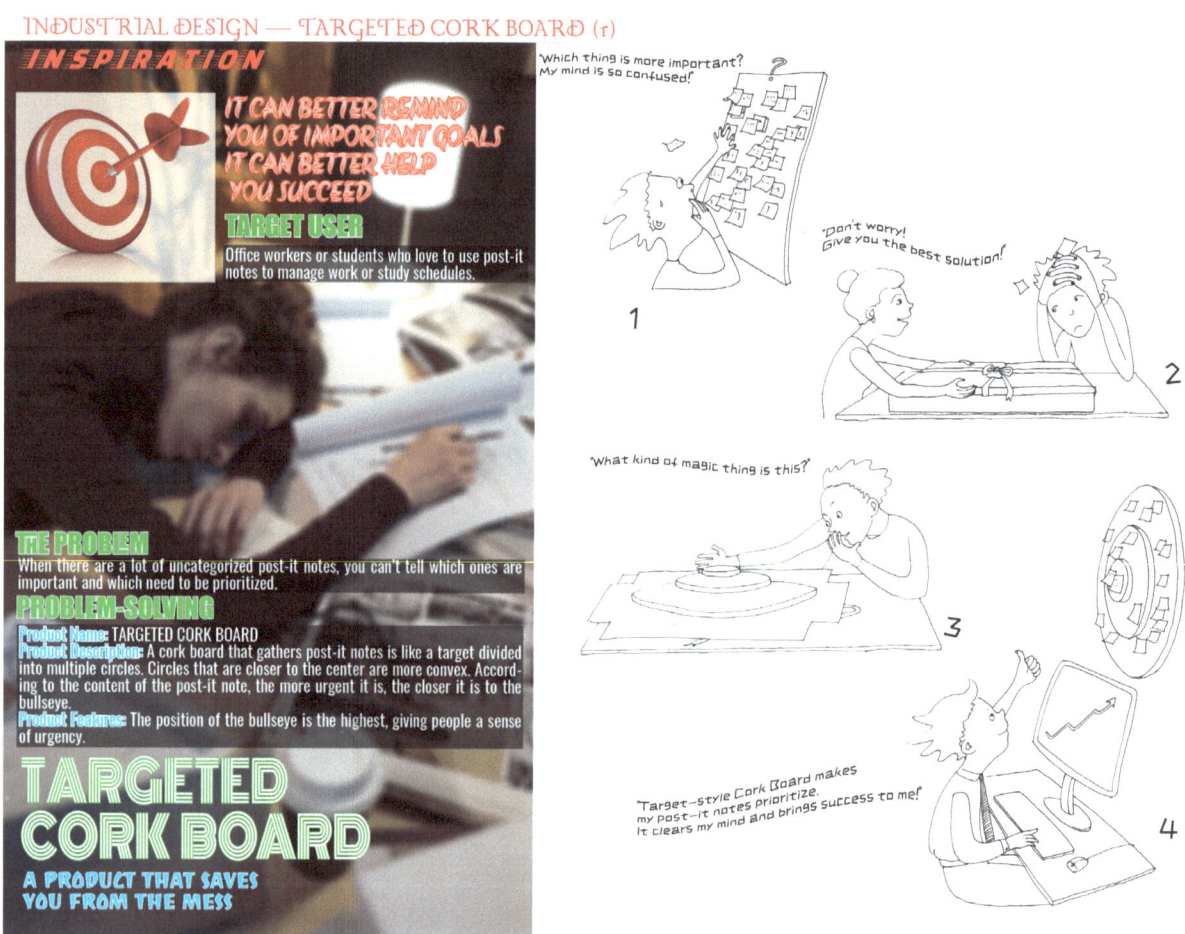

Product Design — Targeted Cork Board (1), digital/ pen on paper, 2022.

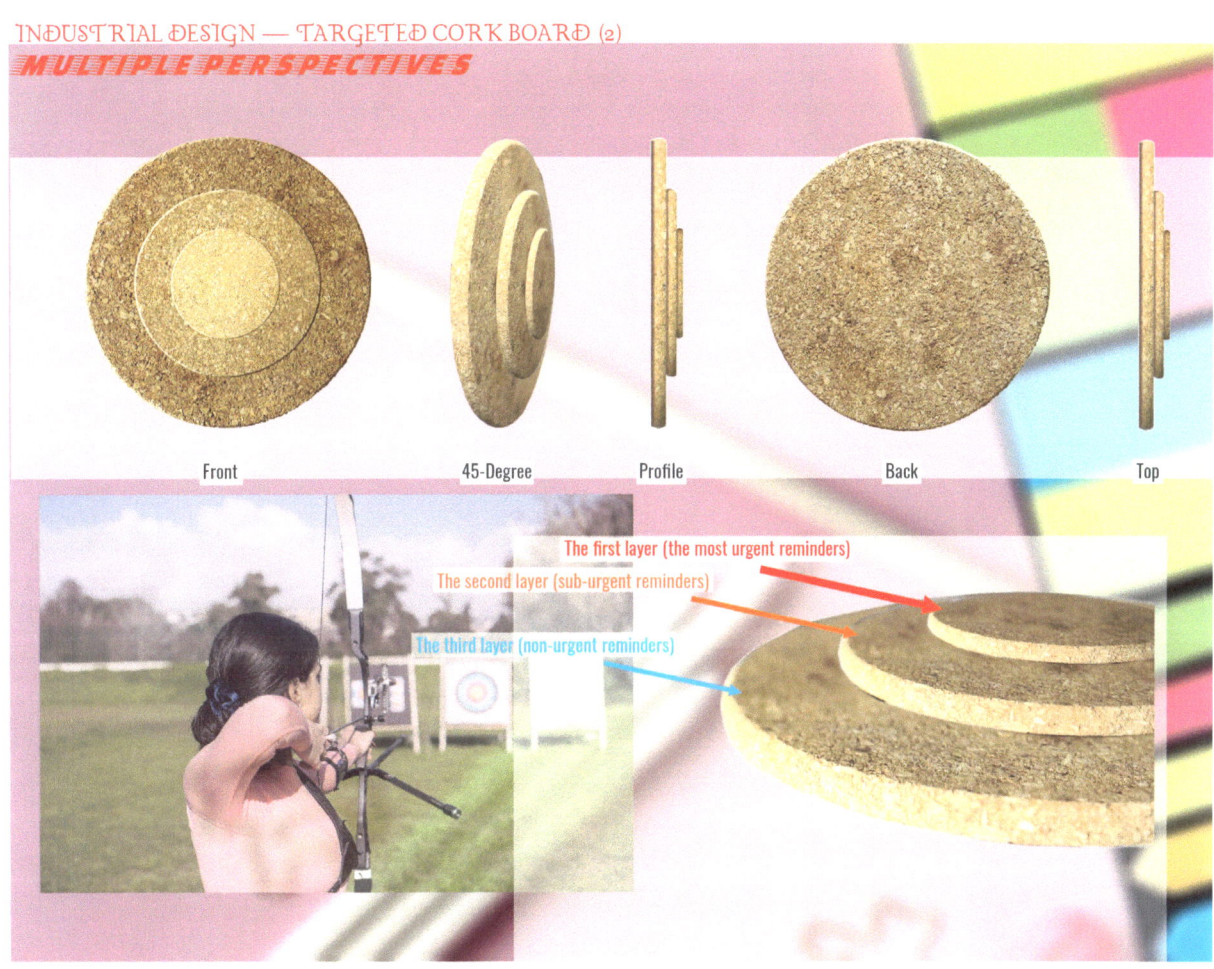

Product Design — Targeted Cork Board (2), digital/ photography, 2022.

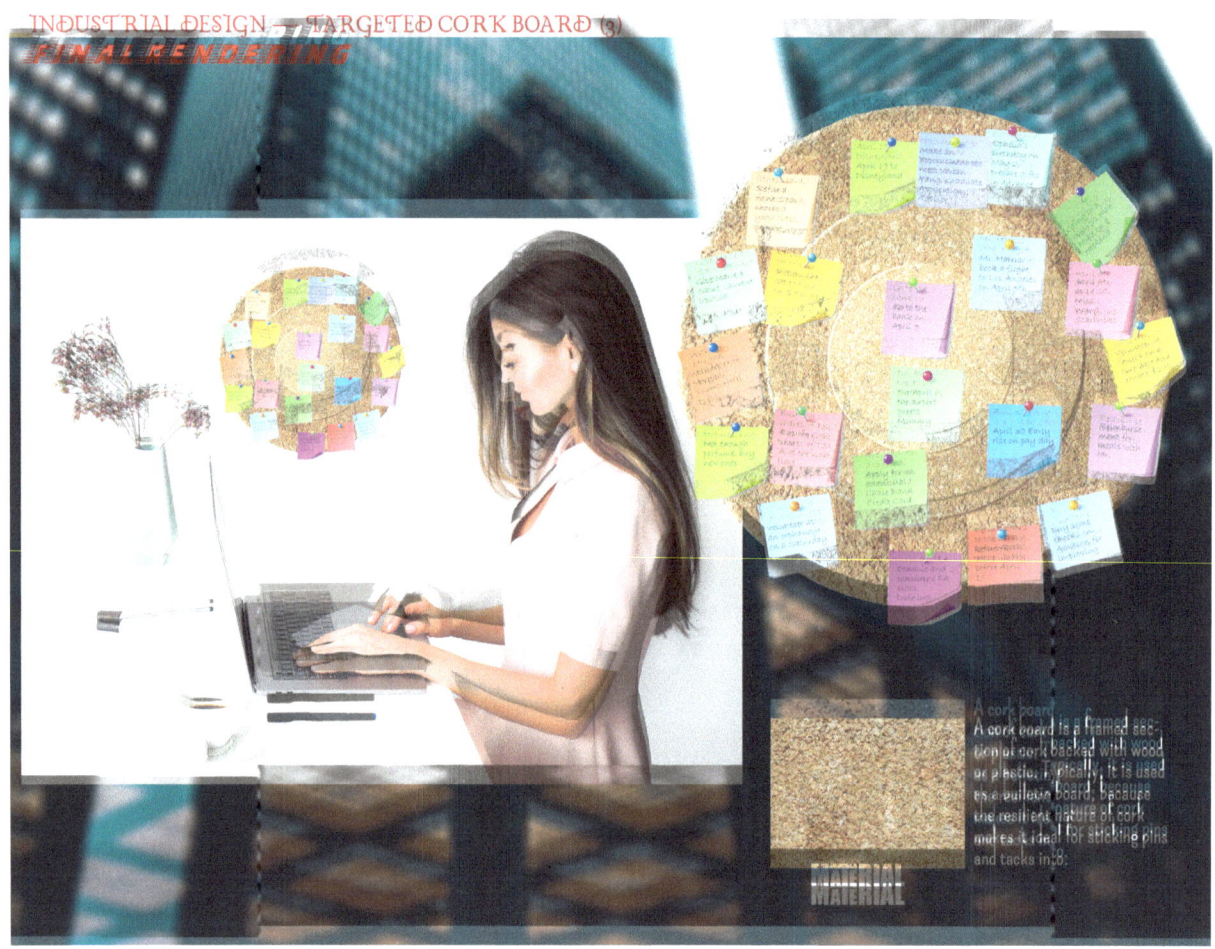

Product Design — Targeted Cork Board (3), digital/ photography, 2022.

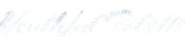

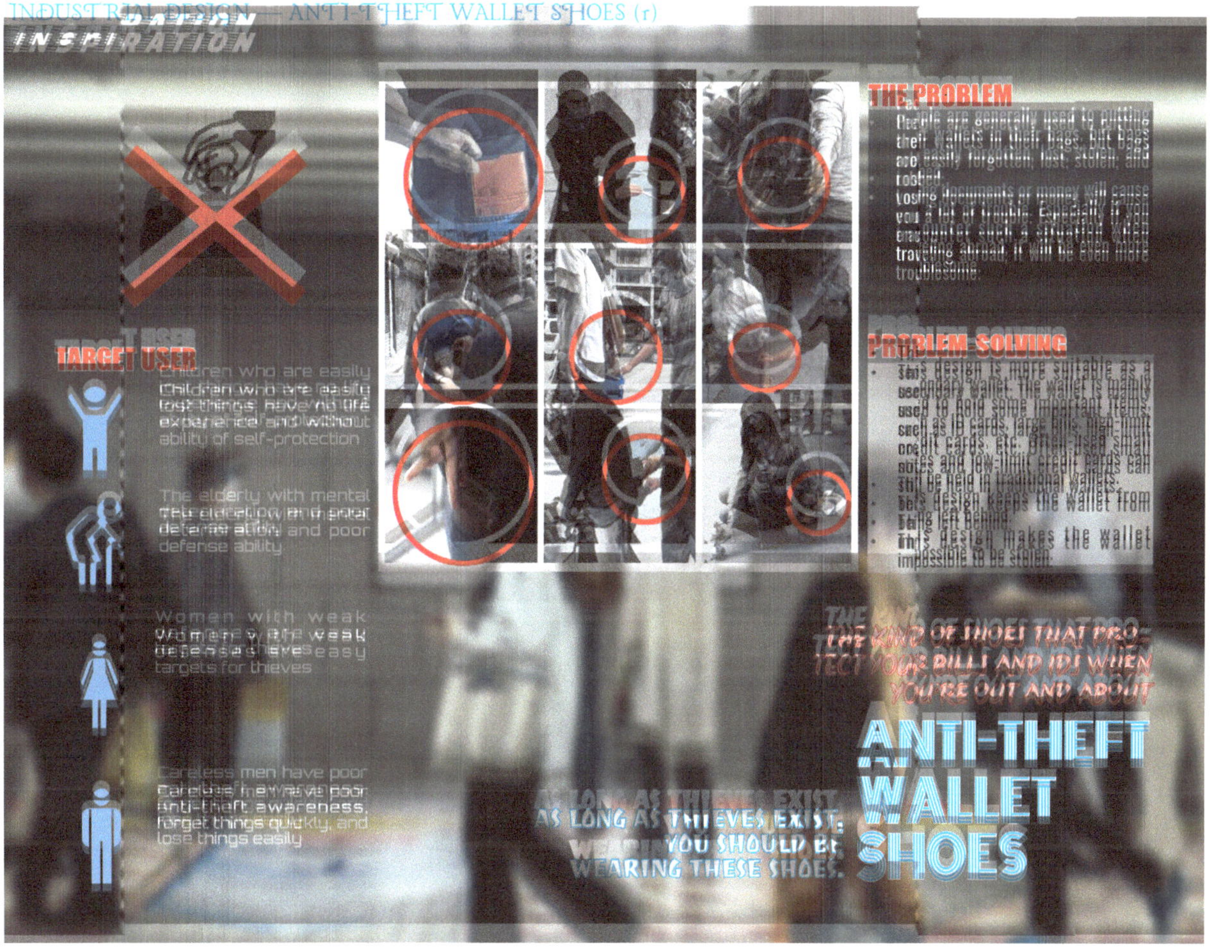

Product Design — Anti-theft Wallet Shoes (1), digital, 2022.

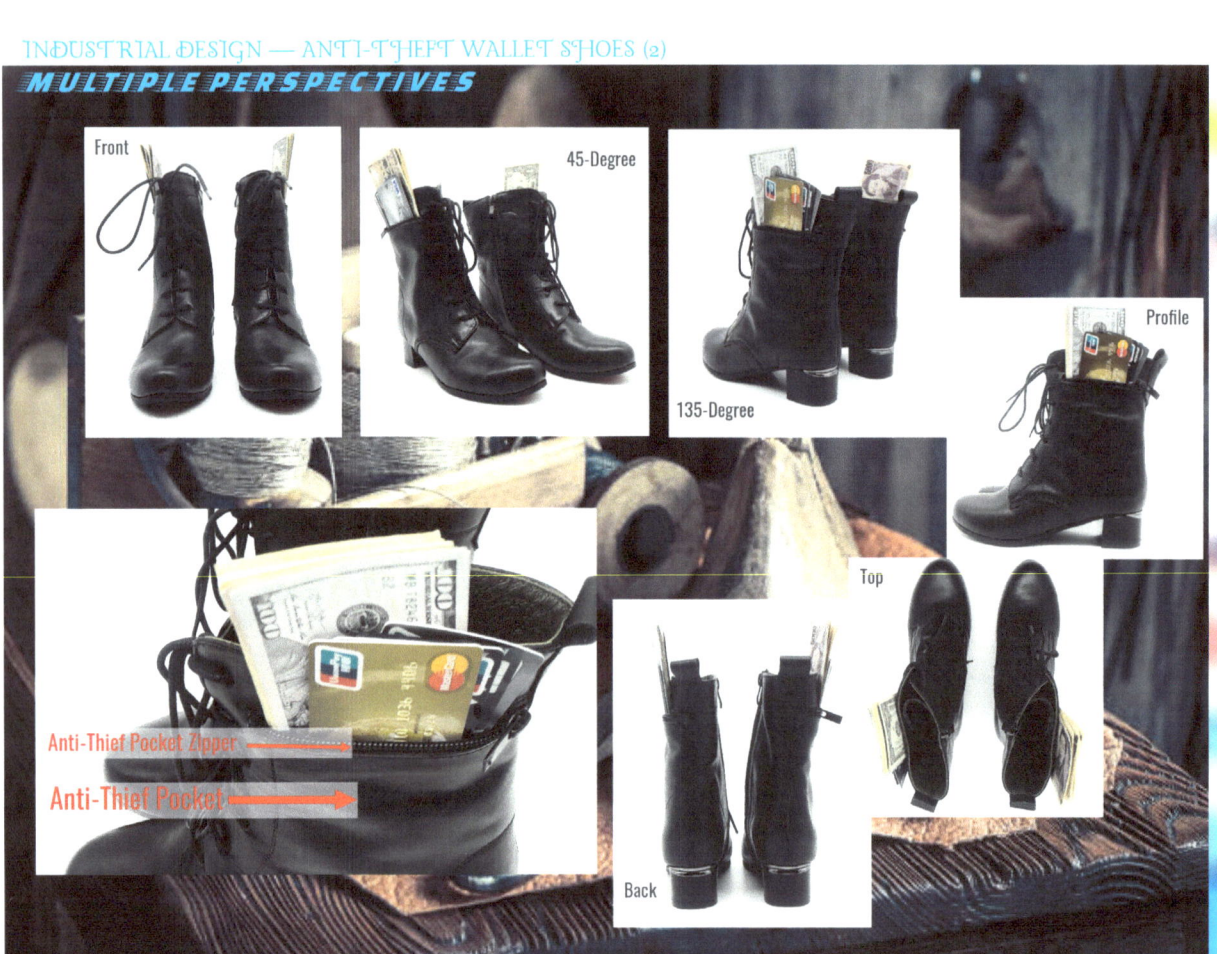

Product Design — Anti-theft Wallet Shoes (2), digital/ leather, 2022.

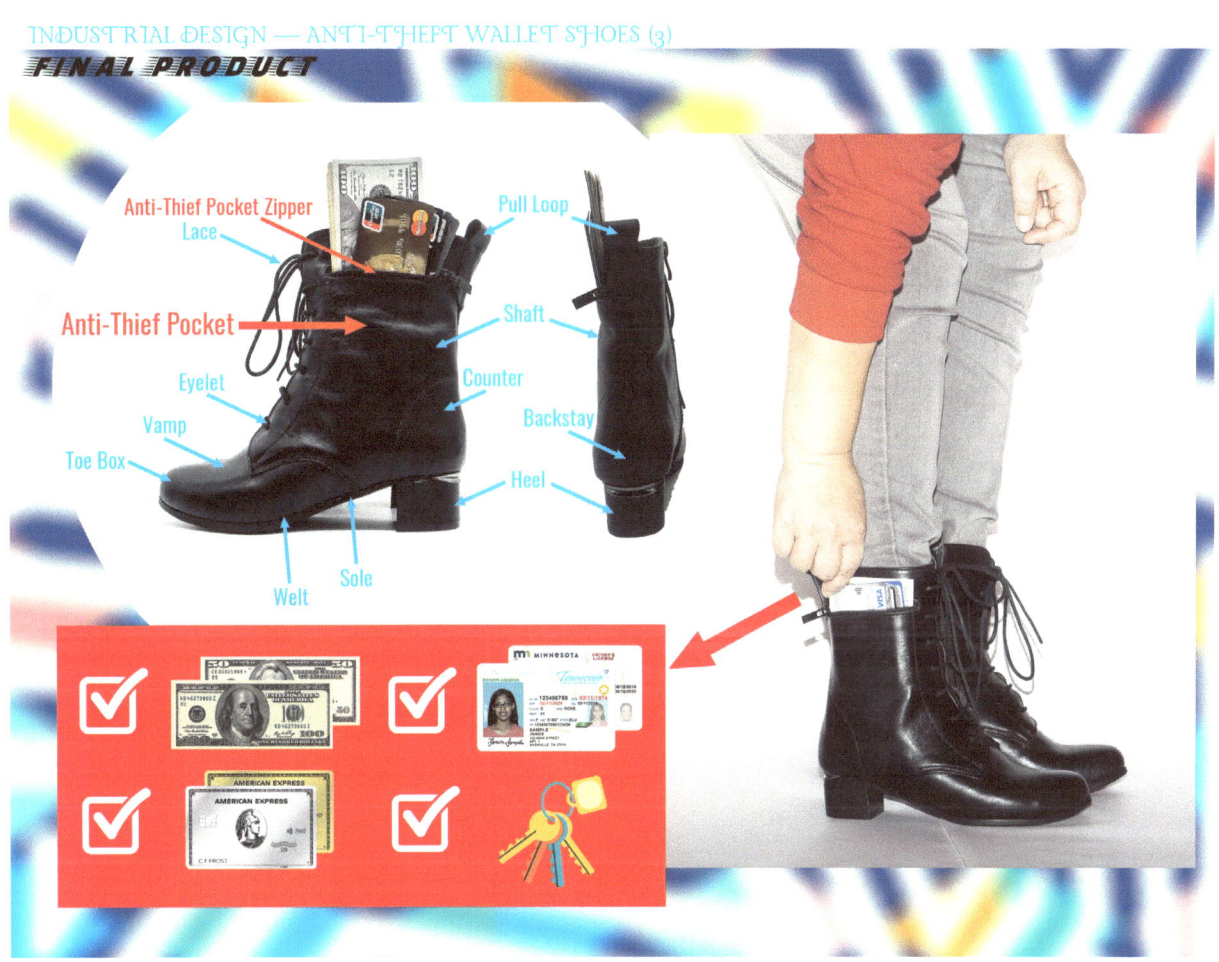

Product Design — Anti-theft Wallet Shoes (3), digital/ leather, 2022.

ZIYAN CHEN
Ruben S. Ayala High School, USA

- Silver Award for Art, 5th Liberty Awards, International Society of Young Artists, USA, 2022.
- Gold Award for Art, 4th Liberty Awards, International Society of Young Artists, USA, 2021.
- Gold Award for Art, 3rd Liberty Awards, International Society of Young Artists, USA, 2020.
- Gold Award for Art, 2nd Liberty Awards, International Society of Young Artists, USA, 2019.

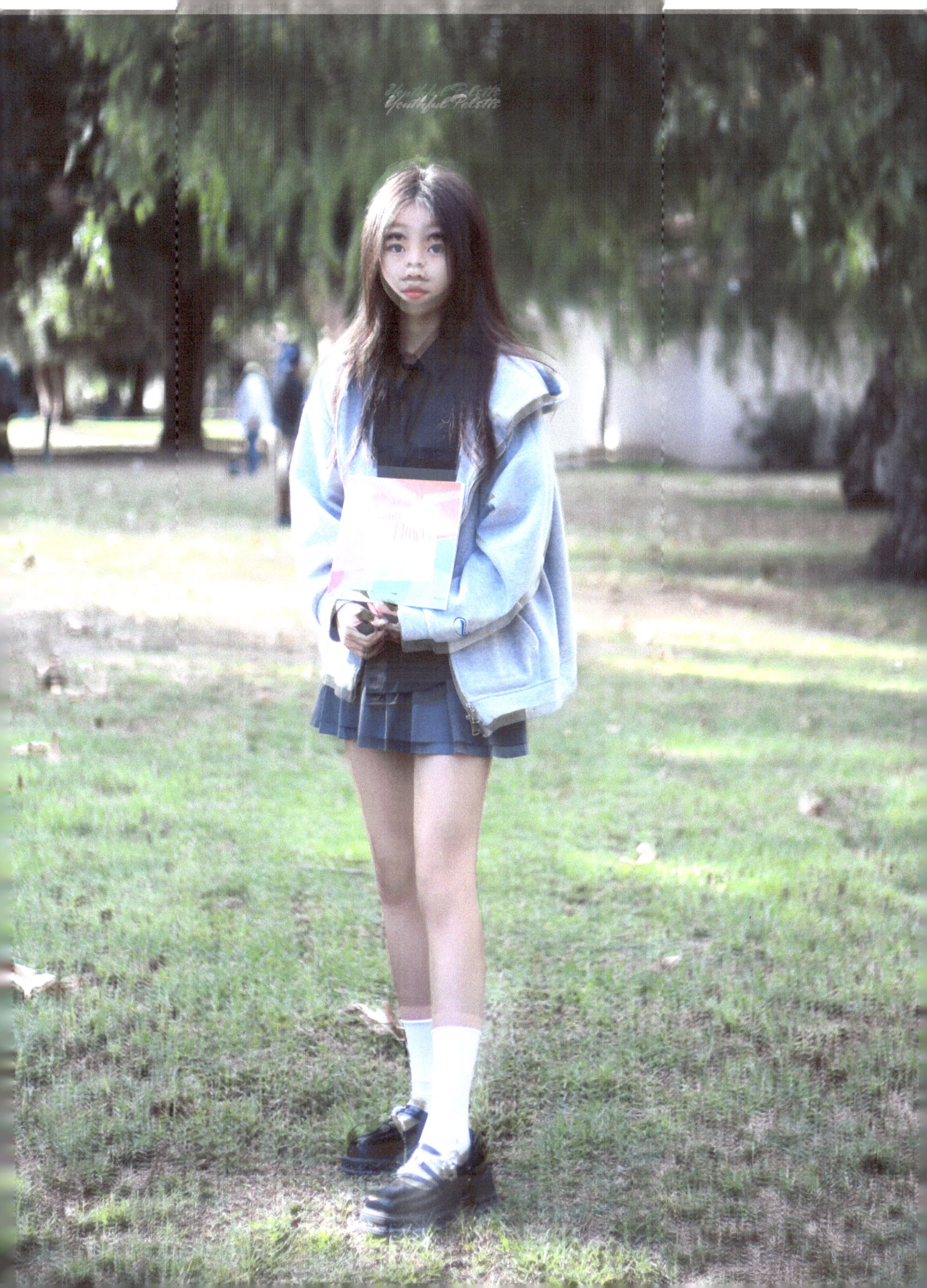

Page Selection in Picture Book *Ineffable Year, Ineffable Flower* (1), digital, 2022.

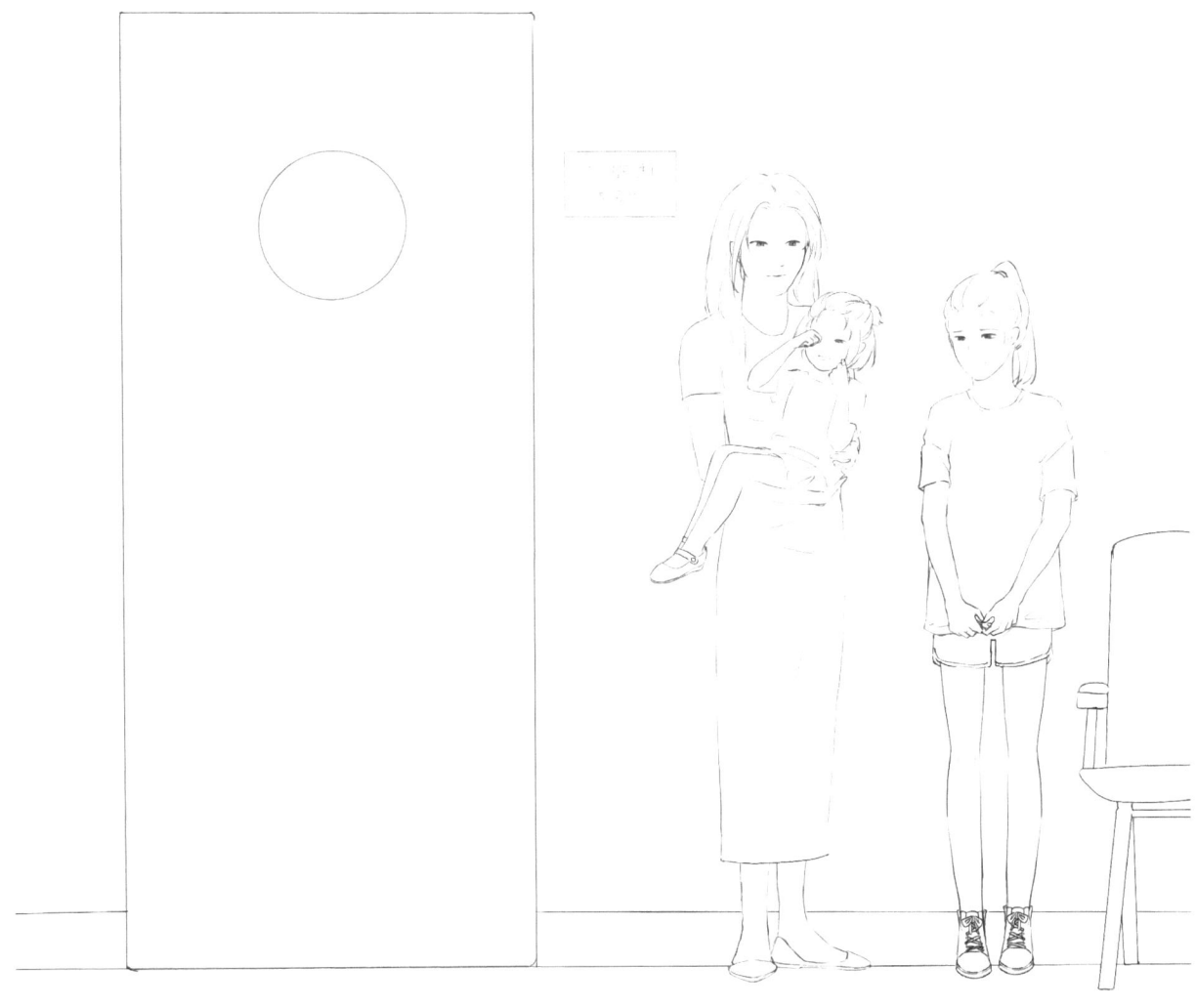

Page Selection in Picture Book *Ineffable Year, Ineffable Flower* (2), digital, 2022.

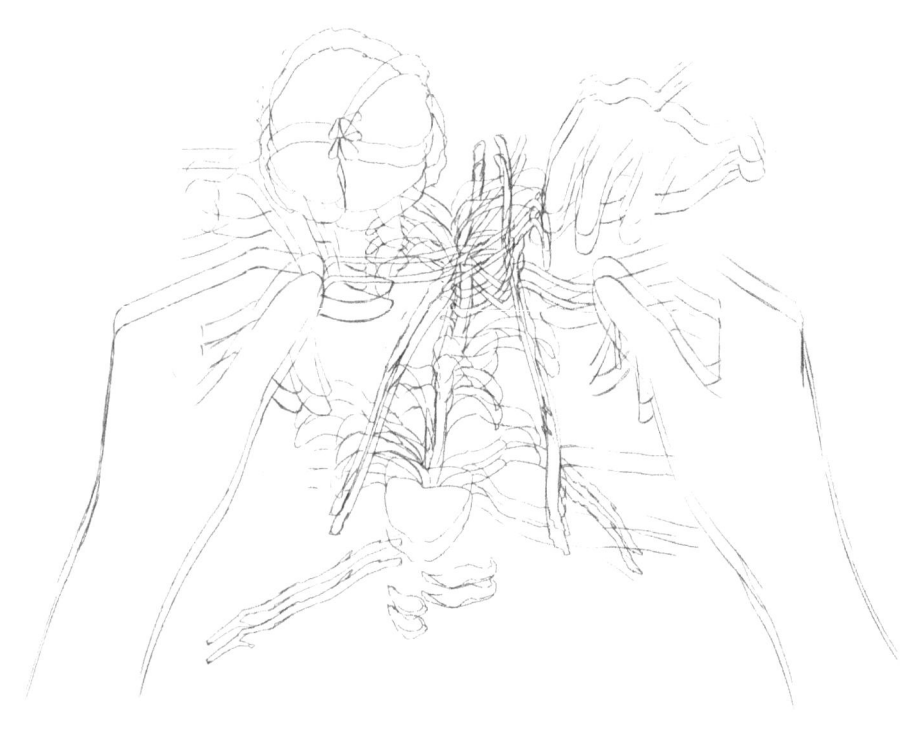

Page Selection in Picture Book *Ineffable Year, Ineffable Flower* (3), digital, 2022.

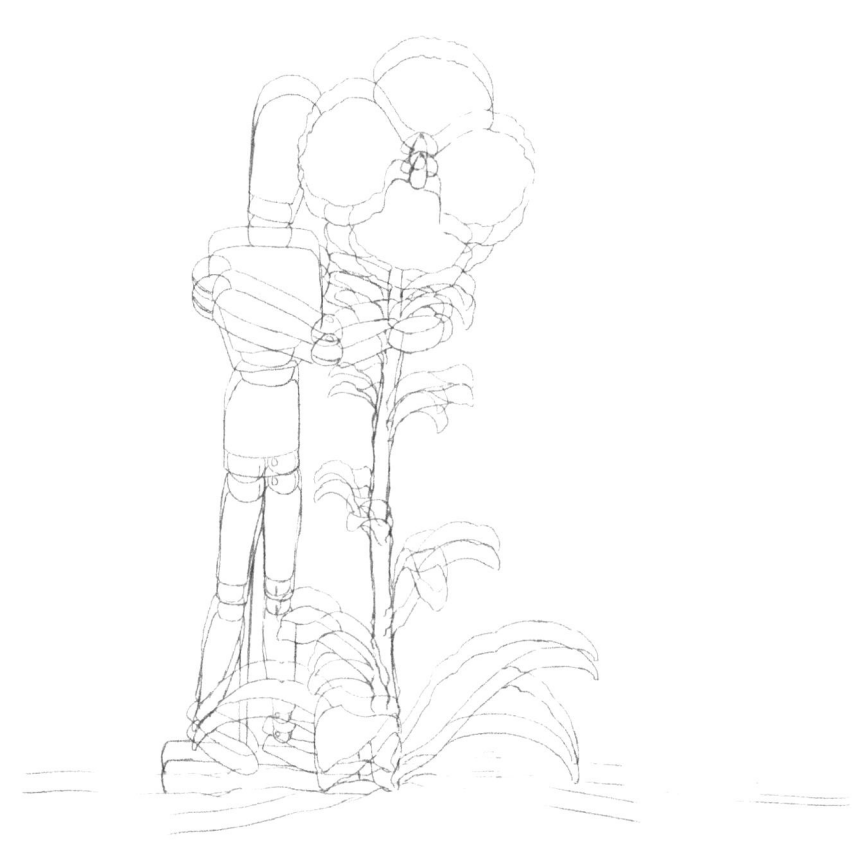

Page Selection in Picture Book *Ineffable Year, Ineffable Flower* (4), digital, 2022.

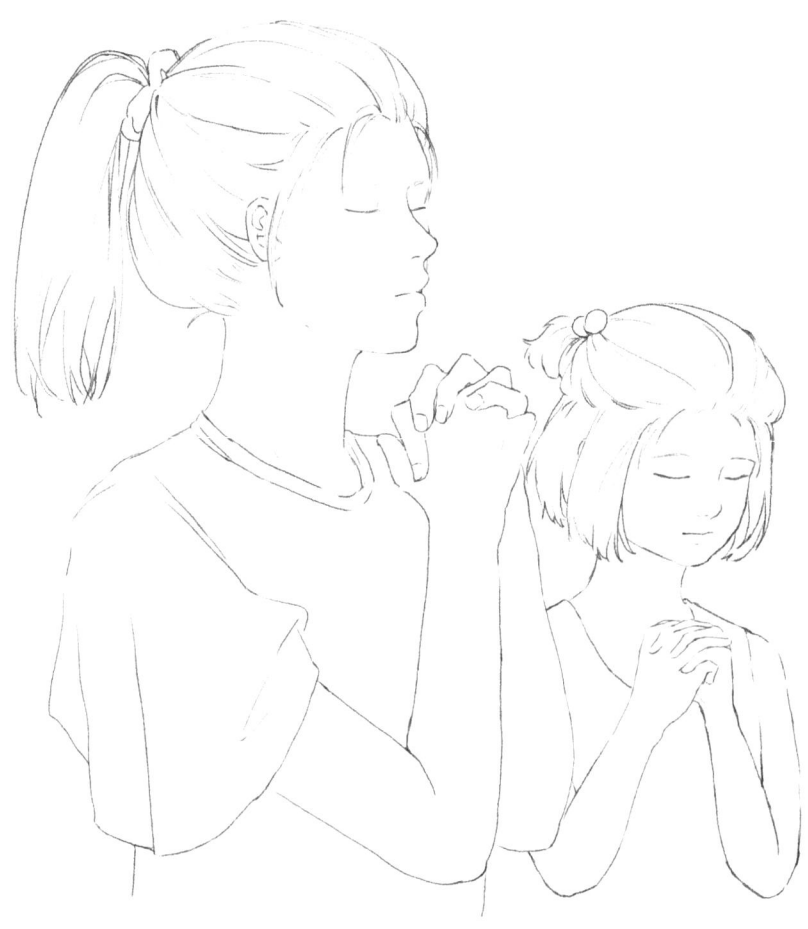

Page Selection in Picture Book *Ineffable Year, Ineffable Flower* (5), digital, 2022.

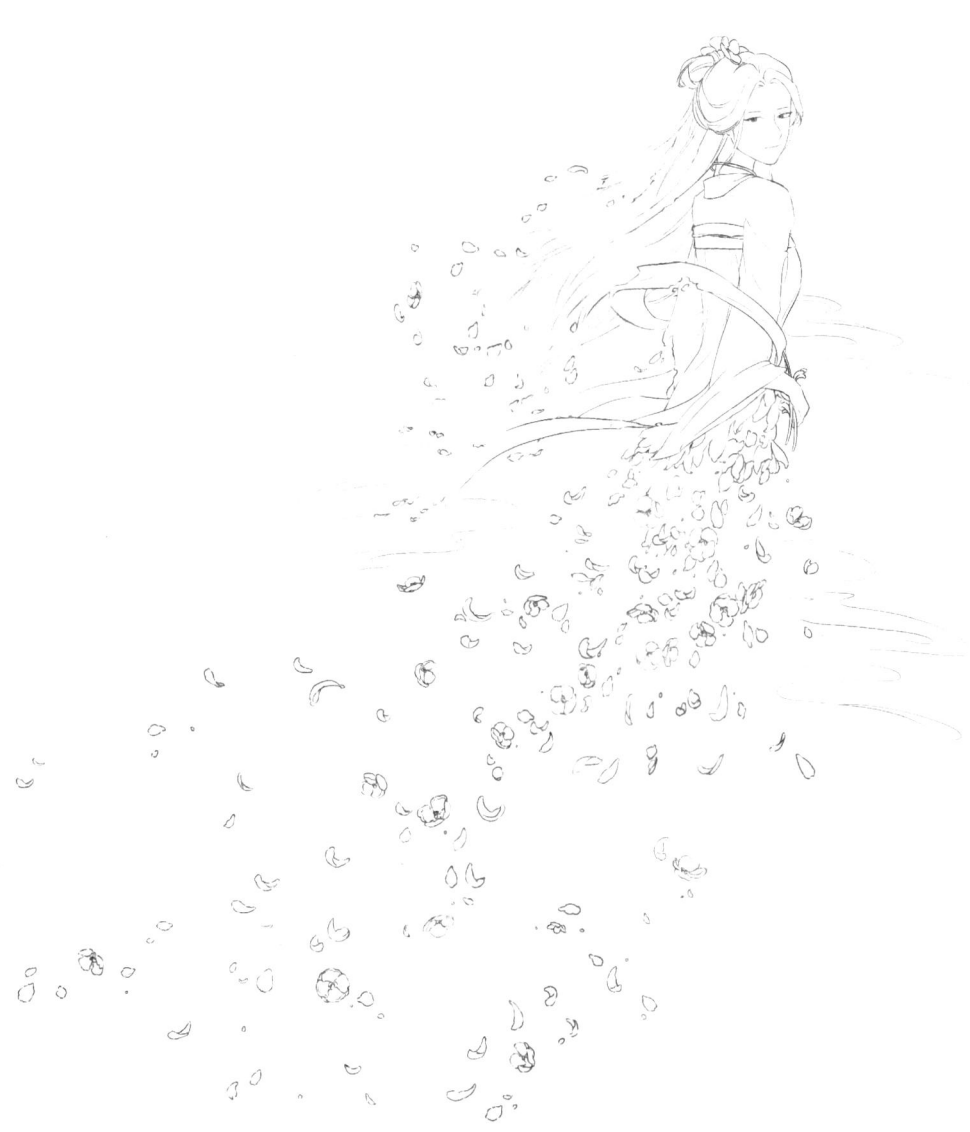

Page Selection in Picture Book *Ineffable Year, Ineffable Flower* (6), digital, 2022.

RONG HONG
CHINA UNIVERSITY OF GEOSCIENCES, WUHAN, CHINA

- Gold Award for Art, 2nd Liberty Awards, International Society of Young Artists, 2019.

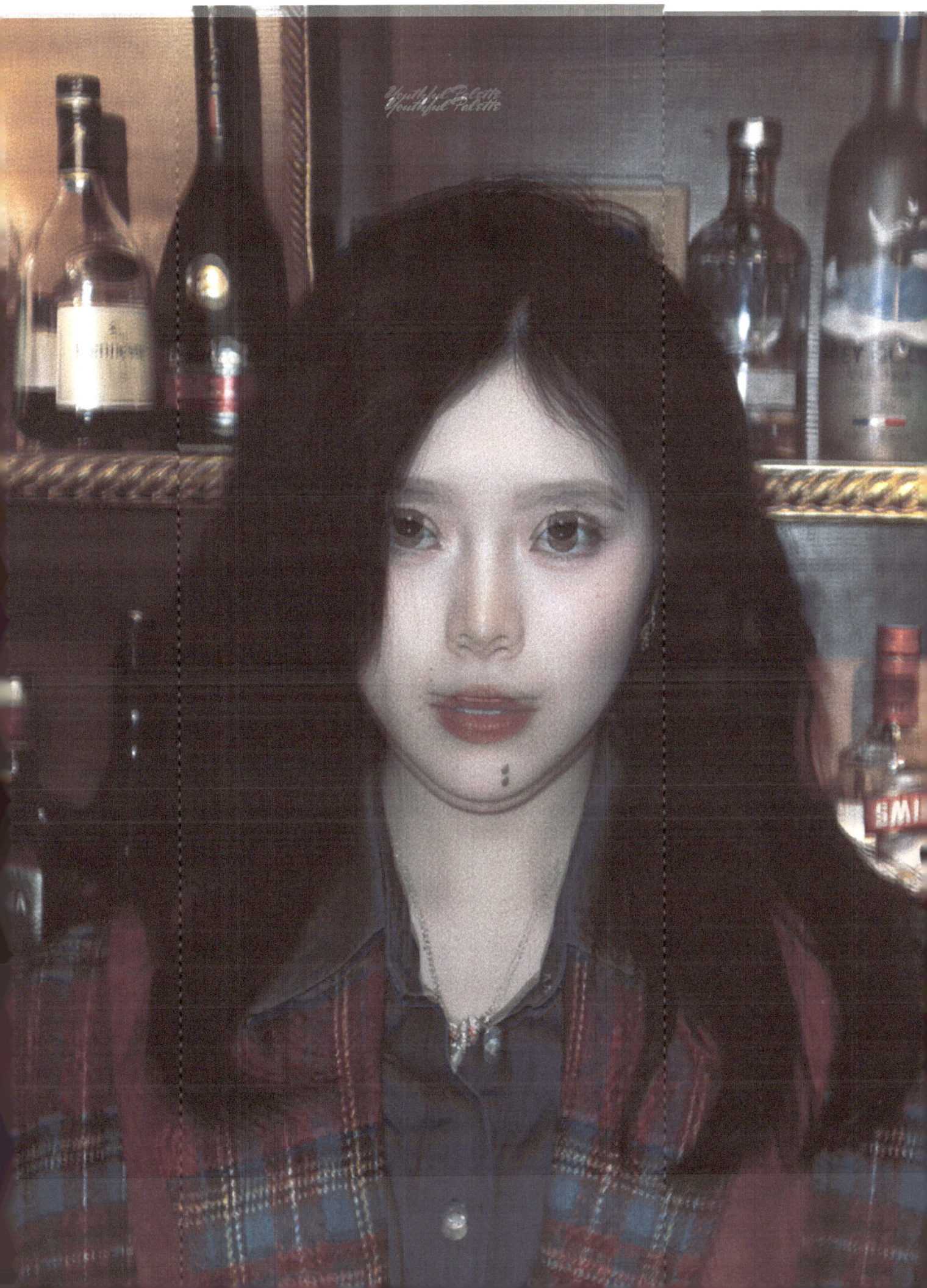

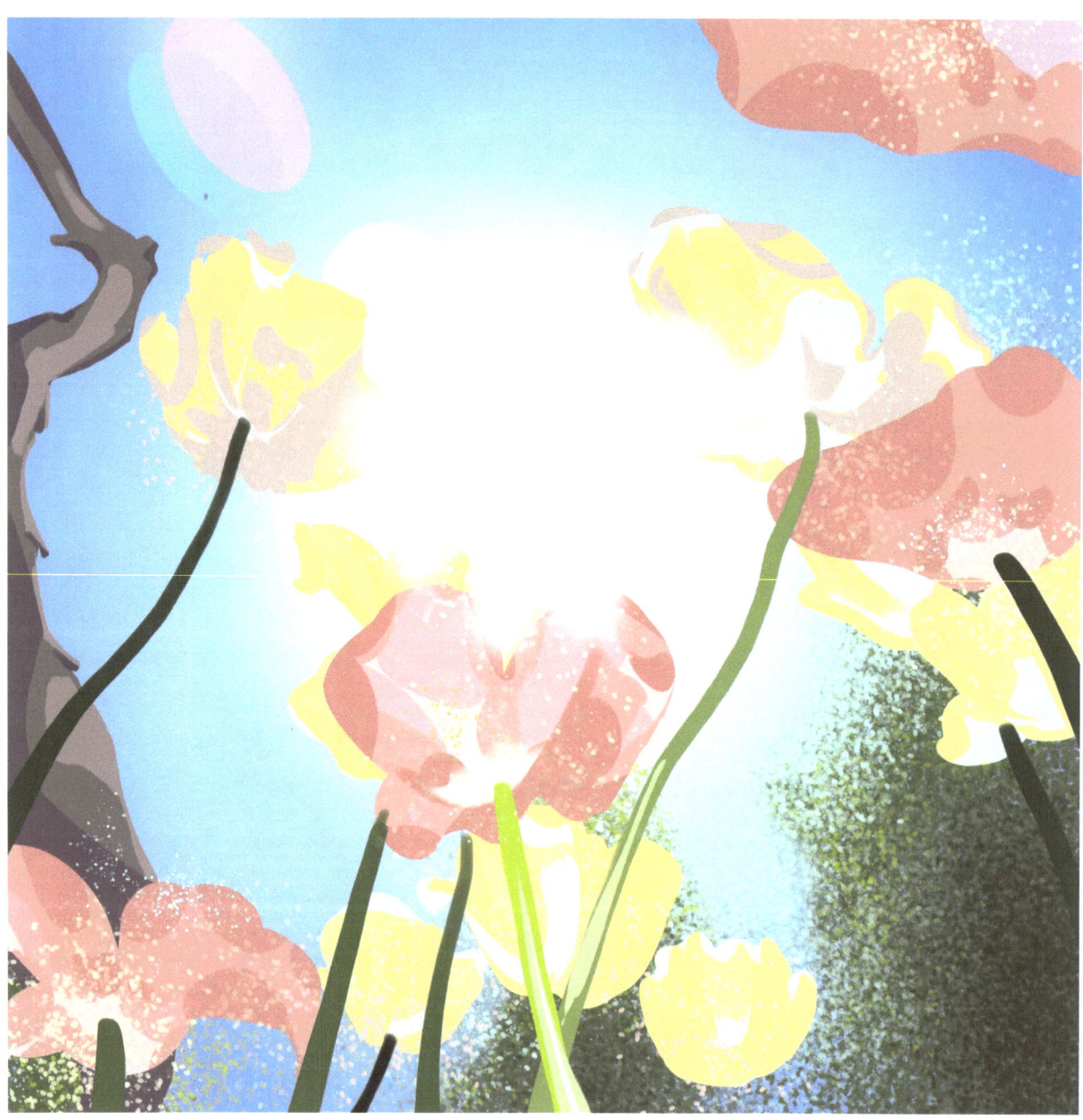

Procreate, digital, 2023.

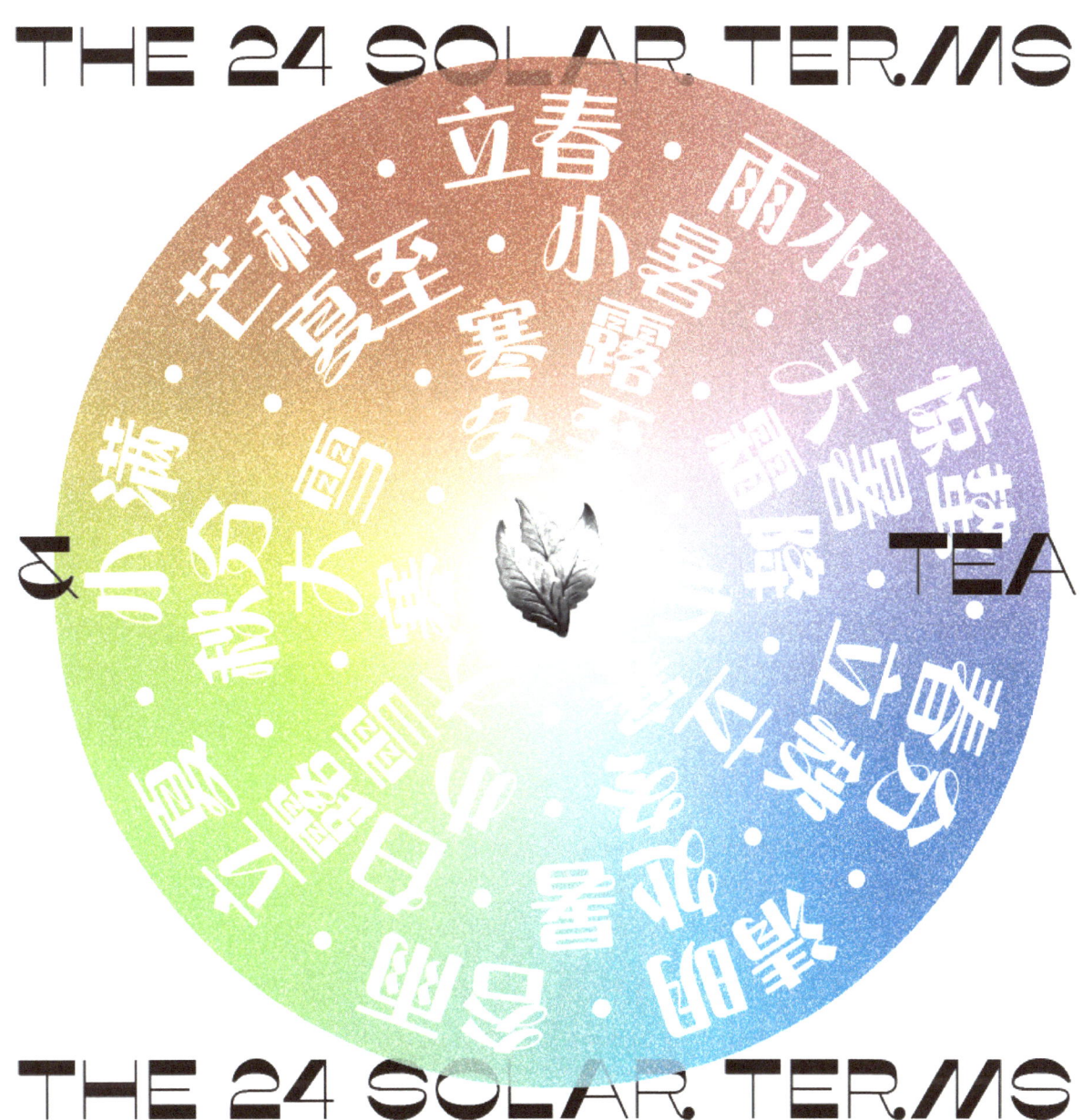

The cover of *The 24 Solar Terms & Tea*, digital, 2023.

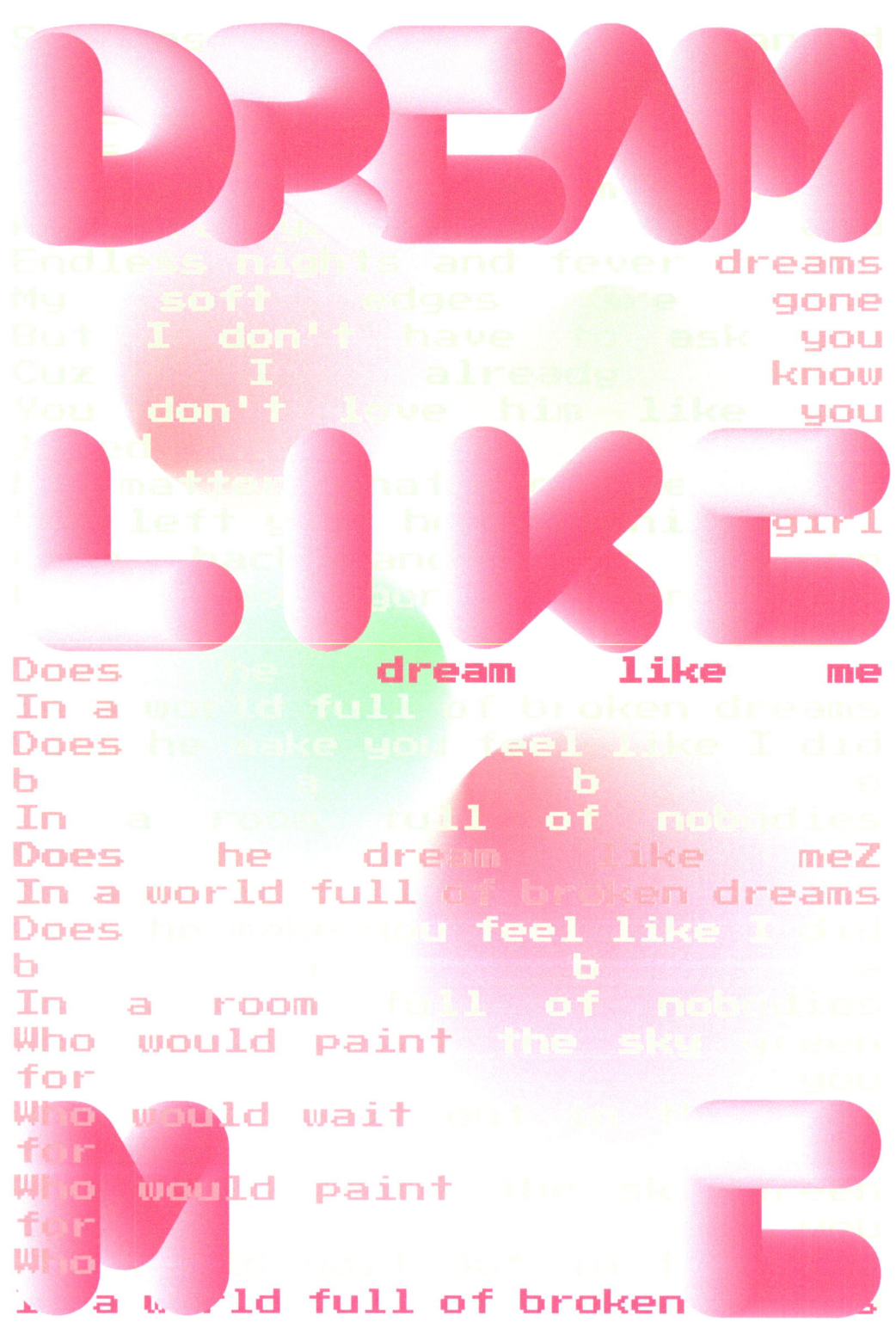

Lyrics Design: *Dream Like Me*, digital, 2023.

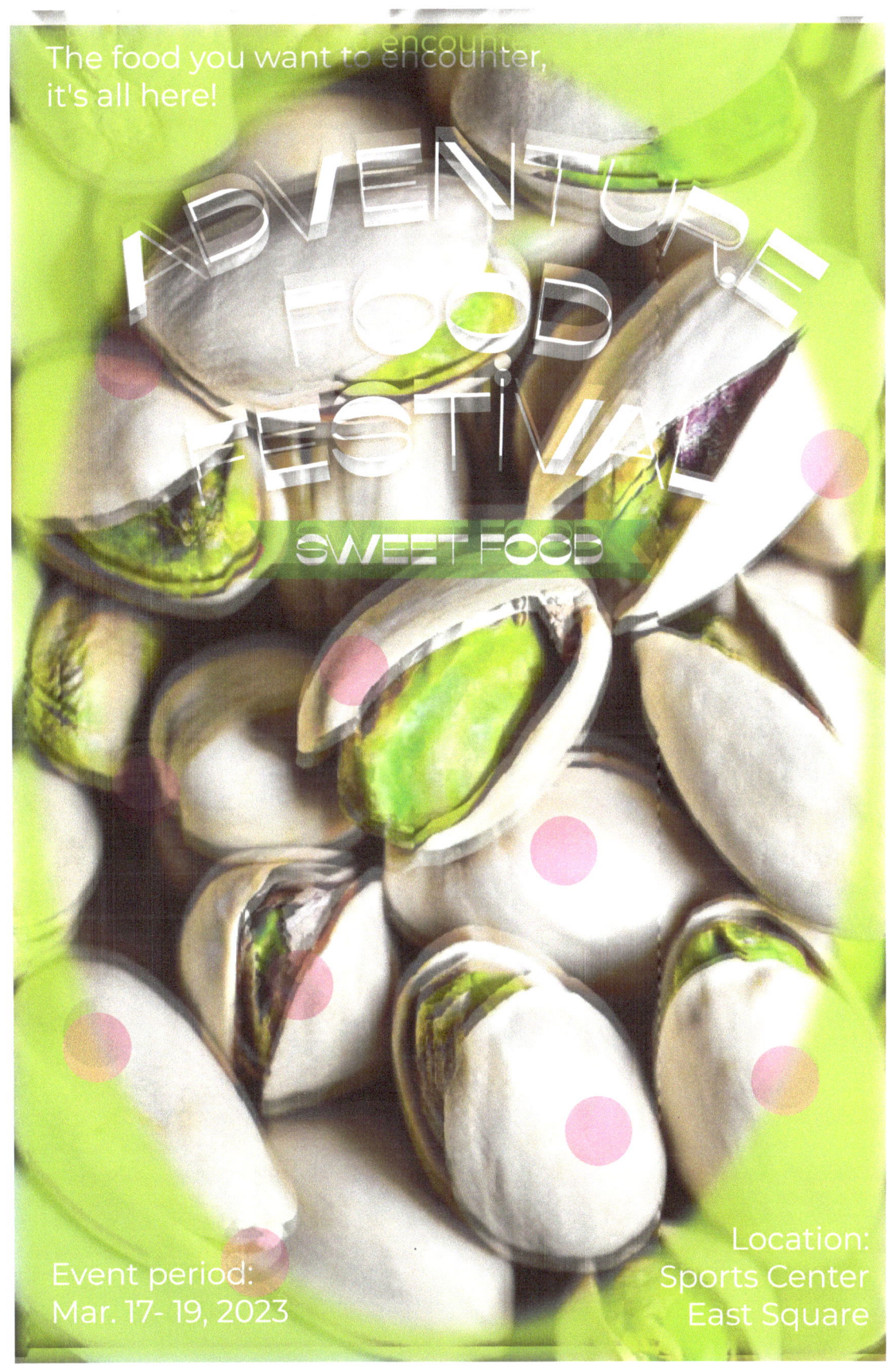

Pistachio special for the Adventure Food Festival poster, digital, 2023.

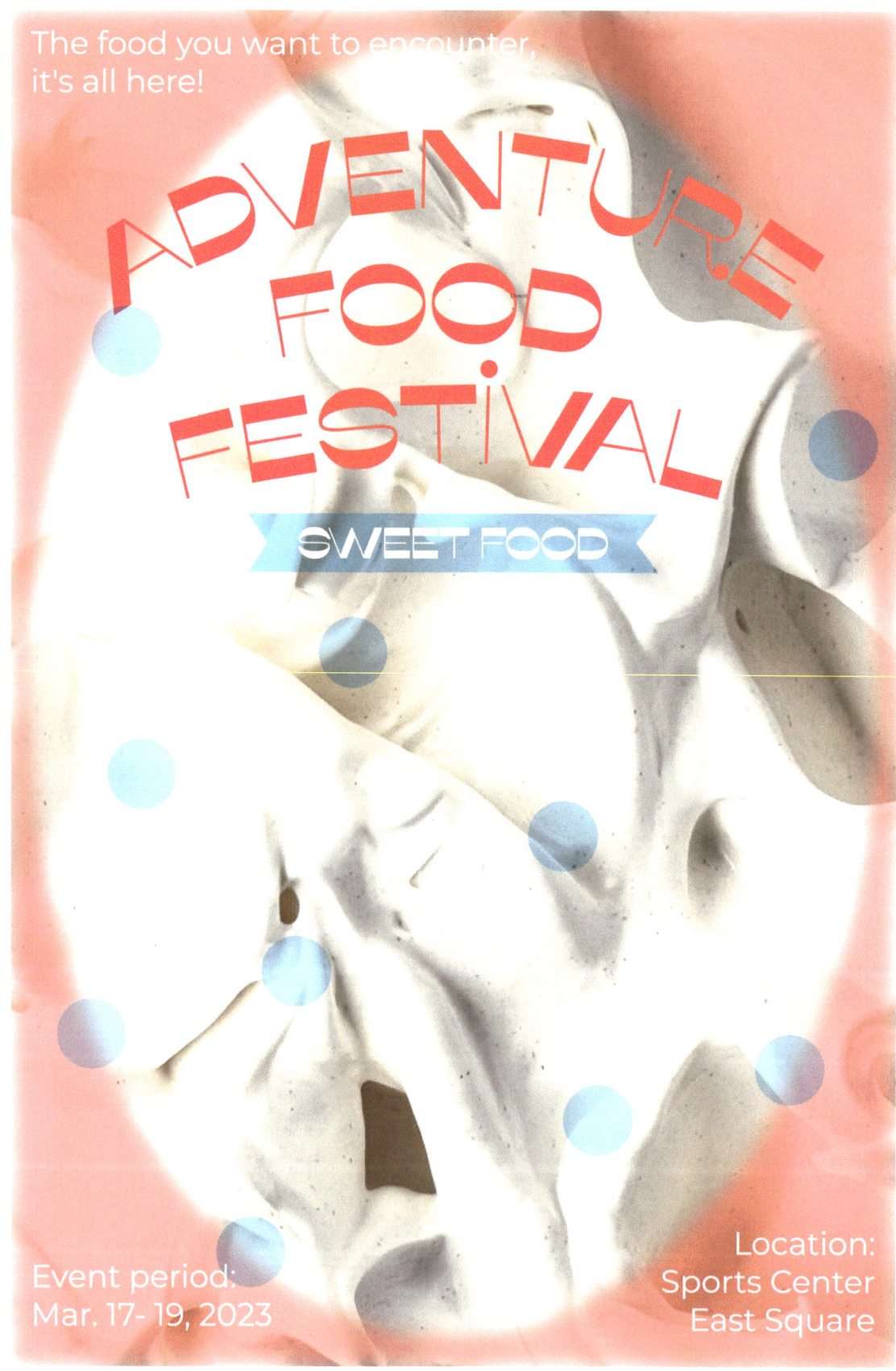

Ice-cream special for the Adventure Food Festival poster, digital, 2023.

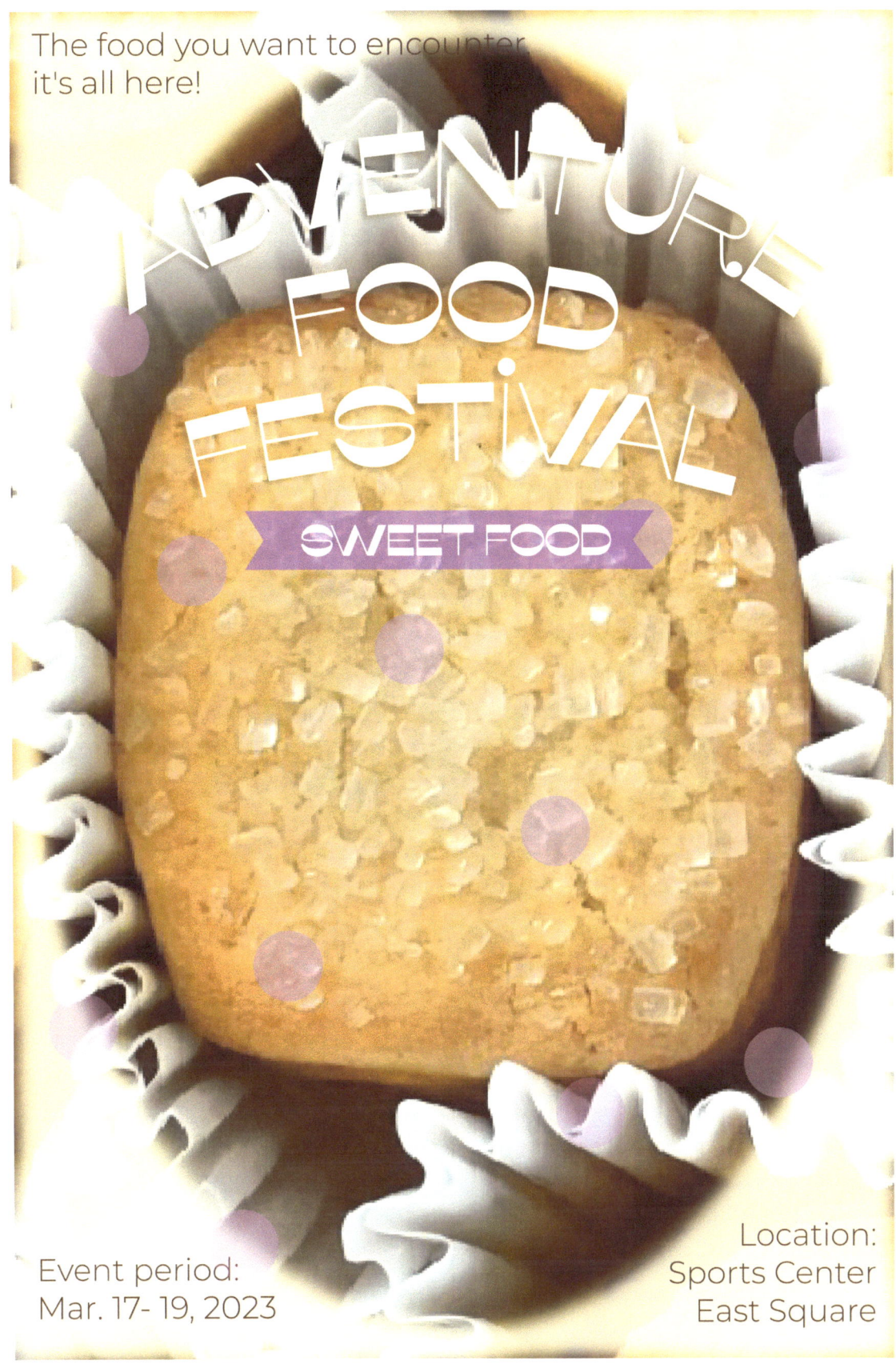

Cookie special for the Adventure Food Festival poster, digital, 2023.

LUJIA GAO
Qingdao No.9 High School, China

- Silver Award for Art, 5th Liberty Awards, International Society of Young Artists, USA, 2022;
- 2nd Prize, National Creative Composition Competition For Secondary School Students, The writing Academy of China, 2022;
- Gold Award for Art, 4th Liberty Awards, International Society of Young Artists, USA, 2021;

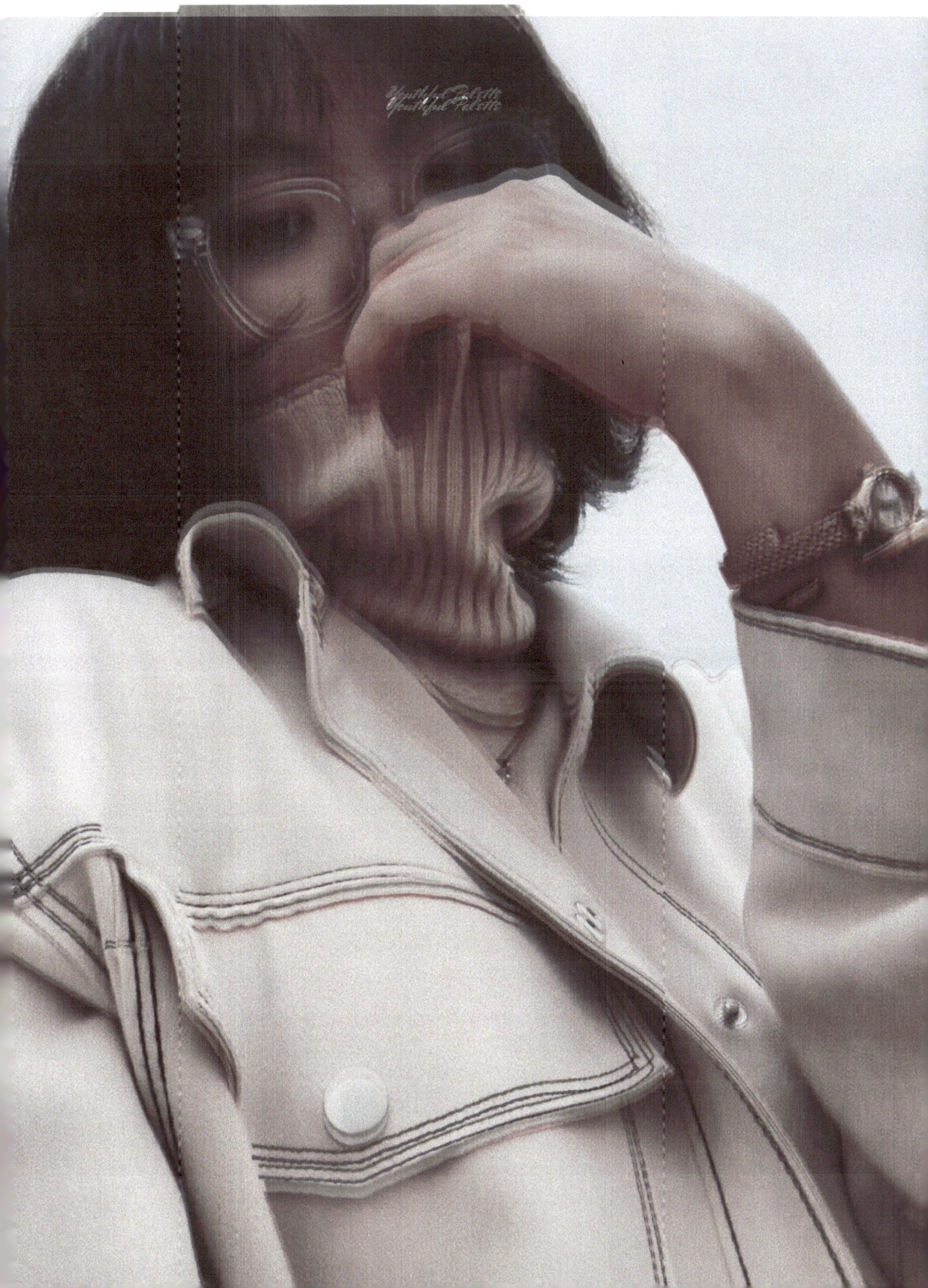

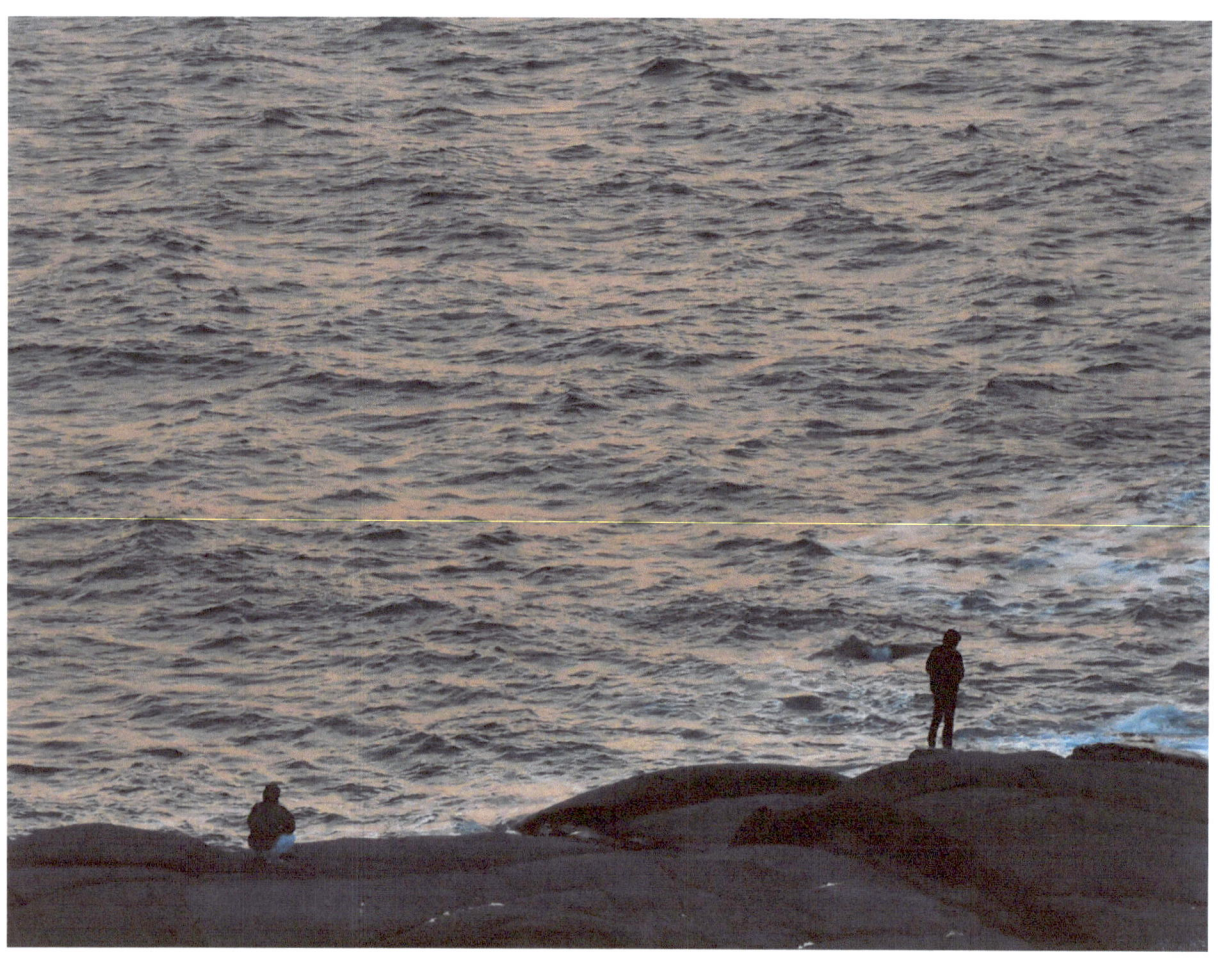

Qingdao No. 1, photography, 2022.

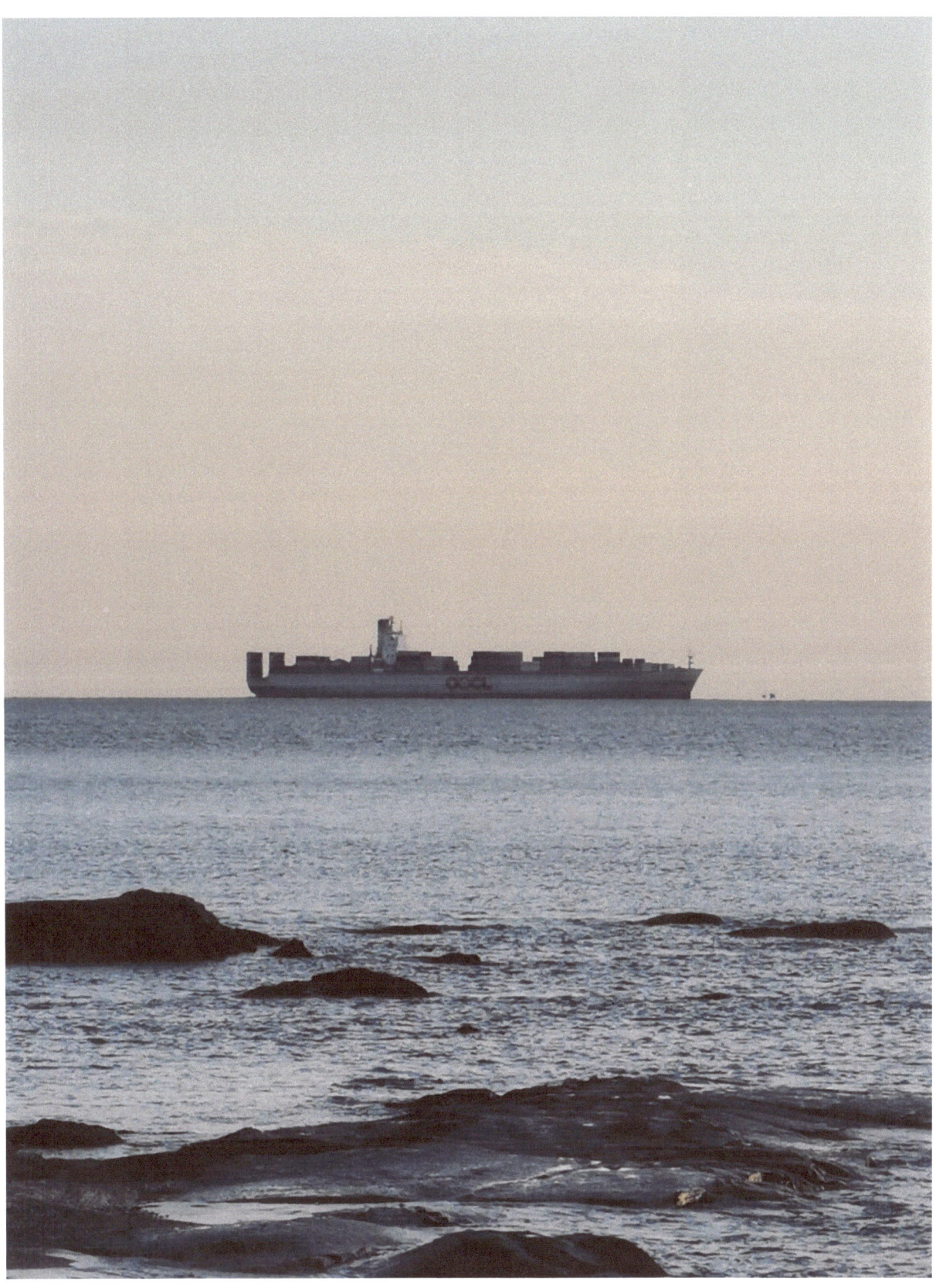

Qingdao No. 2, photography, 2022.

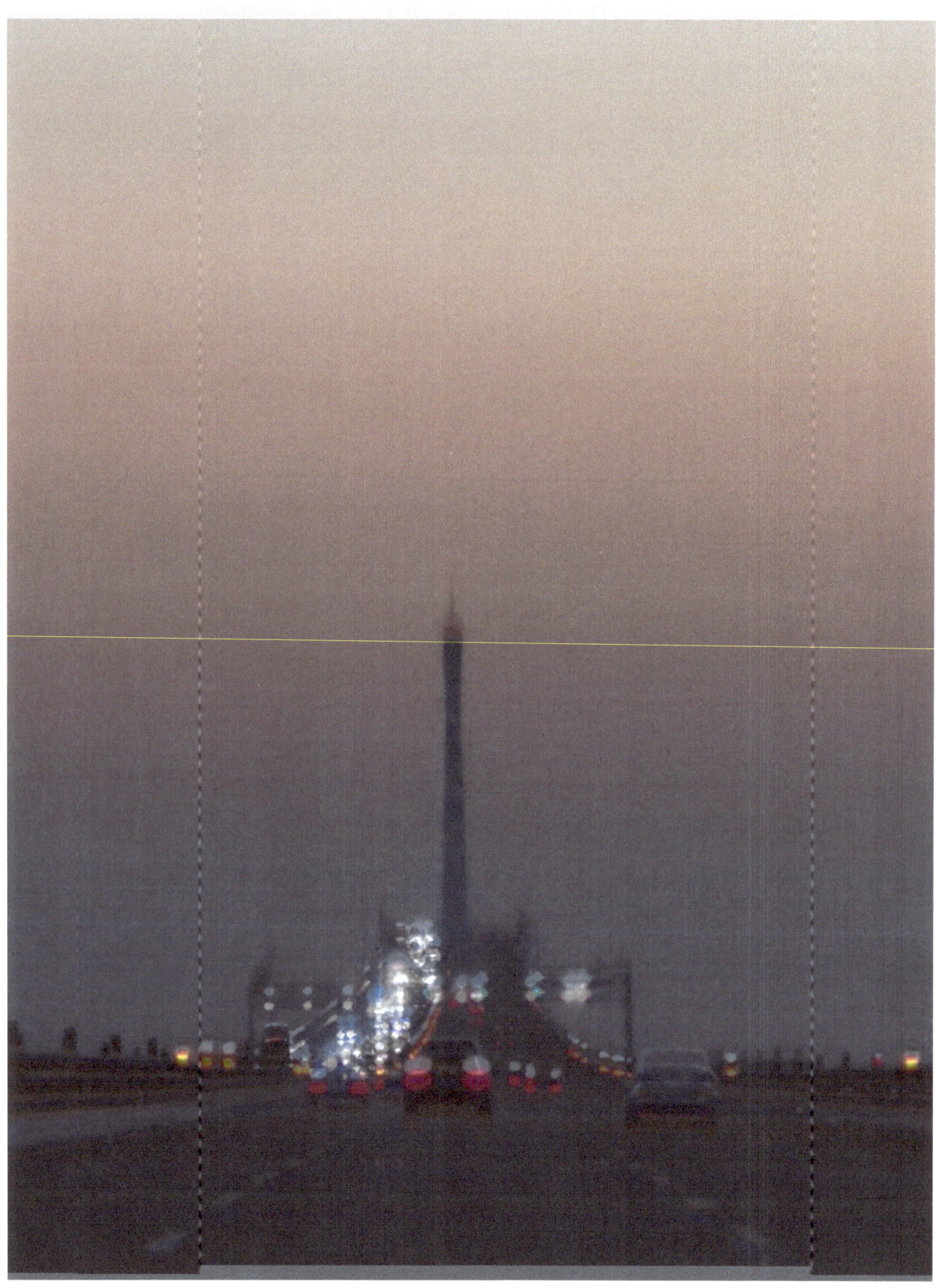

Qingdao No. 5, photography, 2022.

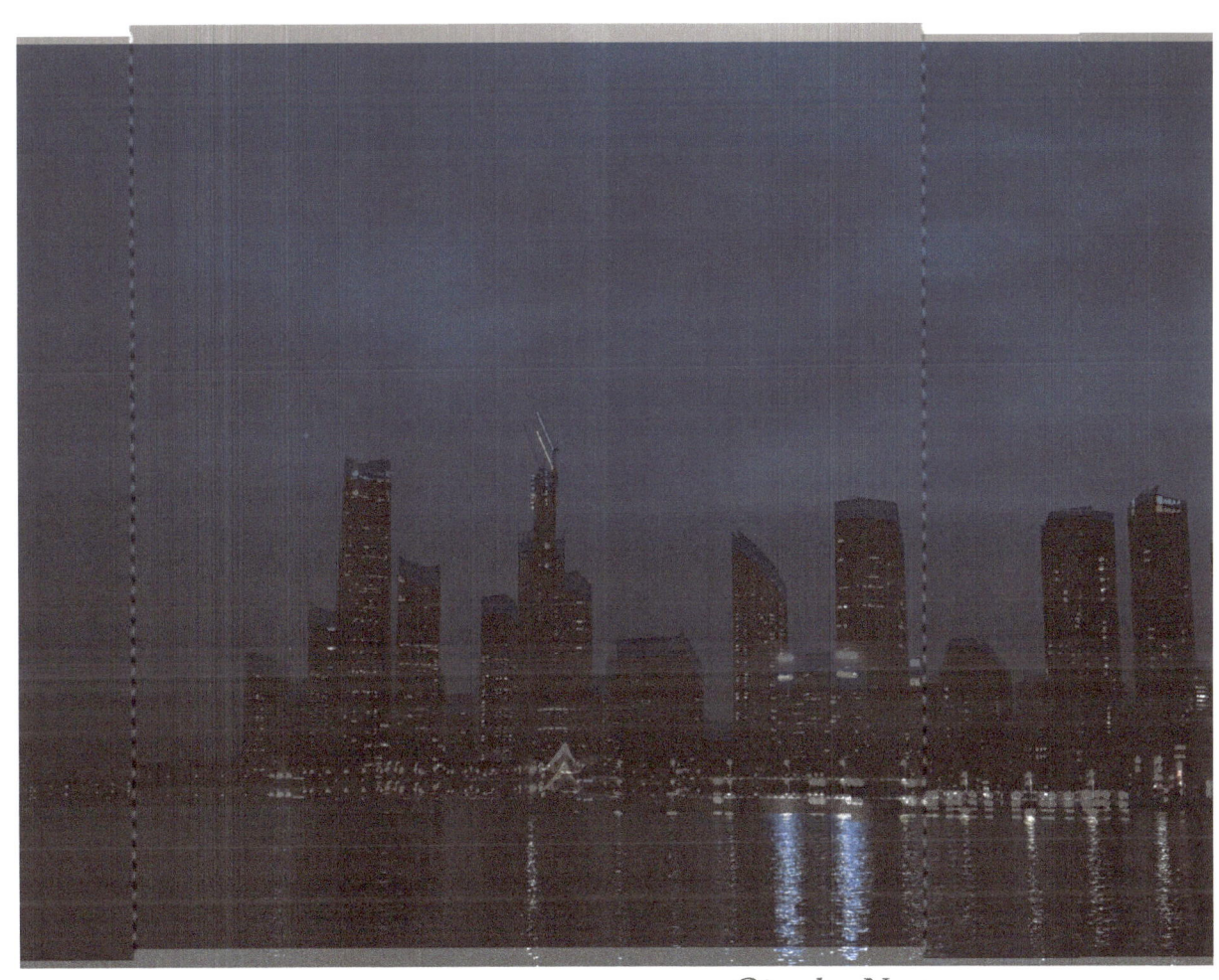

Qingdao No. 6, photography, 2022.

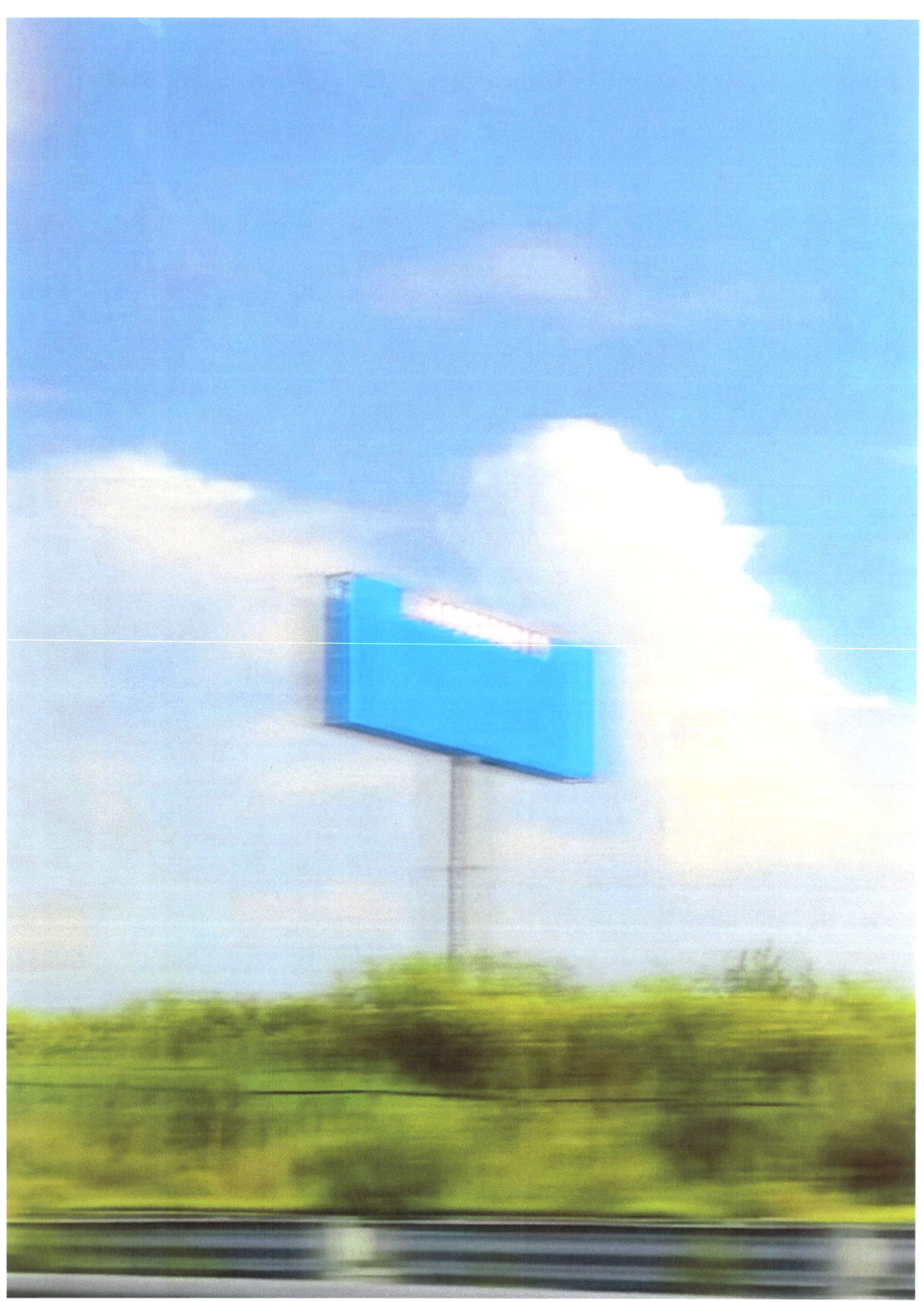

Qingdao No. 7, photography, 2022.

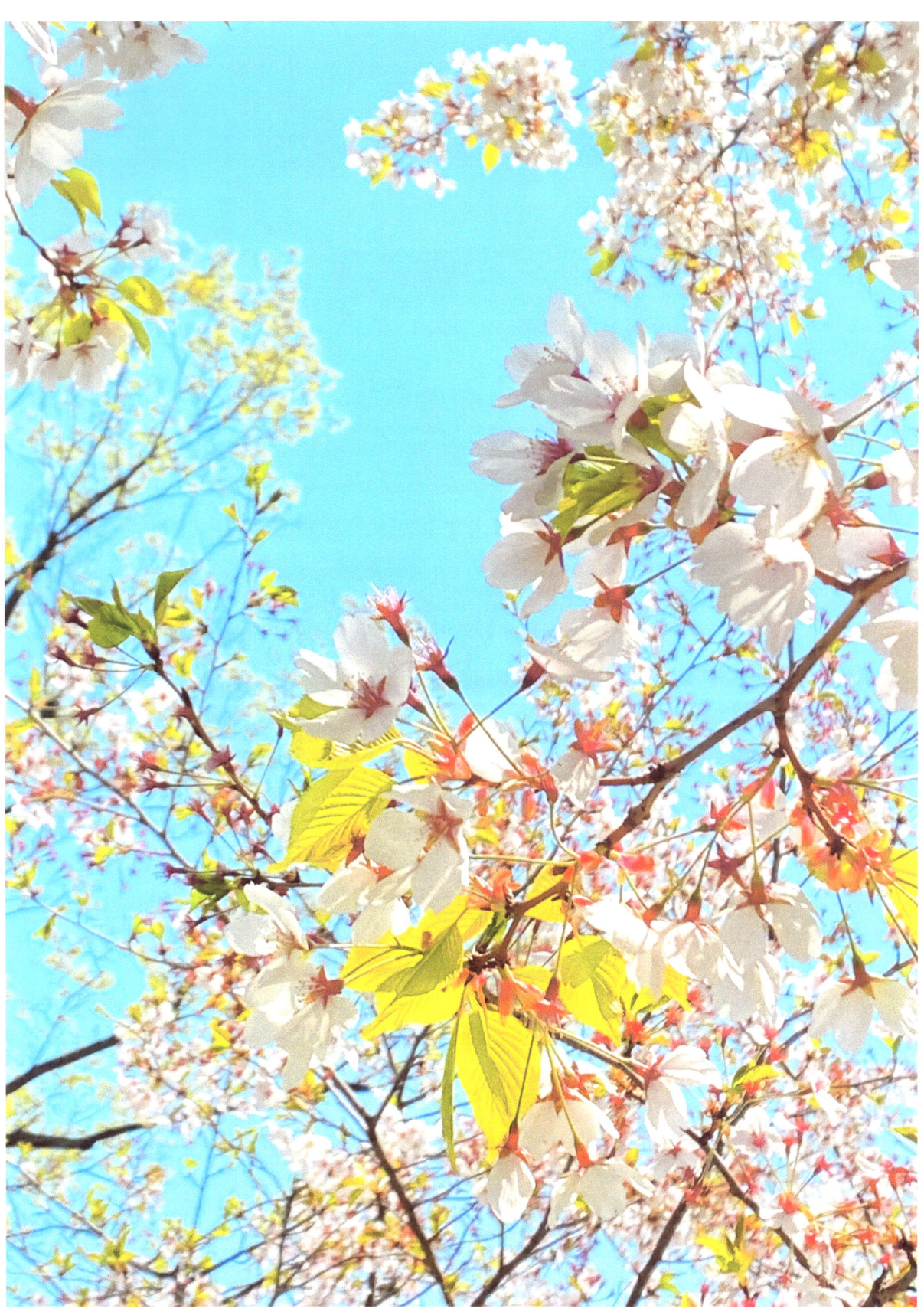

Qingdao No. 8, photography, 2022.

JUNKAI GONG
Princeton High School, NJ, USA

- Bronze Award for Art, 5th Liberty Awards, International Society of Young Artists, USA, 2022.
- Qualified for the Tournament of Champions, USA, 2022.
- Semifinalist (Top 4), the Varsity Lincoln-Douglas Division, 47th University of Pennsylvania Tournament, University of Pennsylvania, USA, 2022.
- Octofinalist (Top 16), the Varsity Lincoln-Douglas Division, Columbia Invitational, Columbia University, USA, 2022.
- 5th Speaker, the Varsity Lincoln-Douglas Division, Columbia Invitational, Columbia University, USA, 2022.
- Triple Octofinalist (Top 64), the Varsity Lincoln-Douglas Division, 48th Annual Harvard National Forensics Tournament, Harvard University, USA, 2022.
- Quarterfinalist (Top 8), the Varsity Lincoln-Douglas Division, Columbia Invitational, Columbia University, USA, 2021.
- Gold Award for Art, 4th Liberty Awards, International Society of Young Artists, USA, 2021
- Double Octofinalist (Top 32), the Varsity Lincoln-Douglas Division, The Princeton Classic, Princeton University, USA, 2021.
- Double Octofinalist (Top 32), the Varsity Lincoln-Douglas Division, The Mid America Cup, Valley High School, USA, 2021.

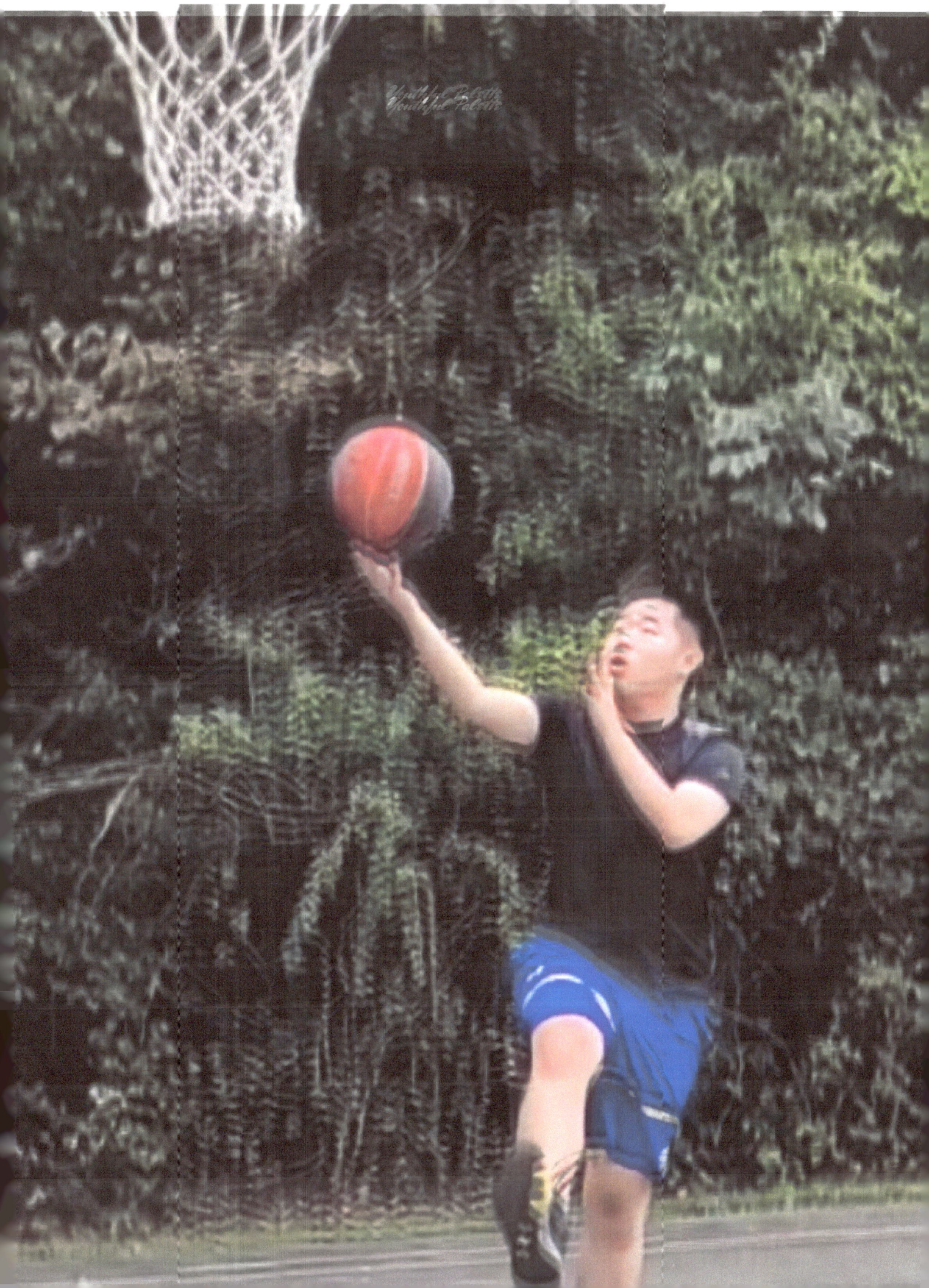

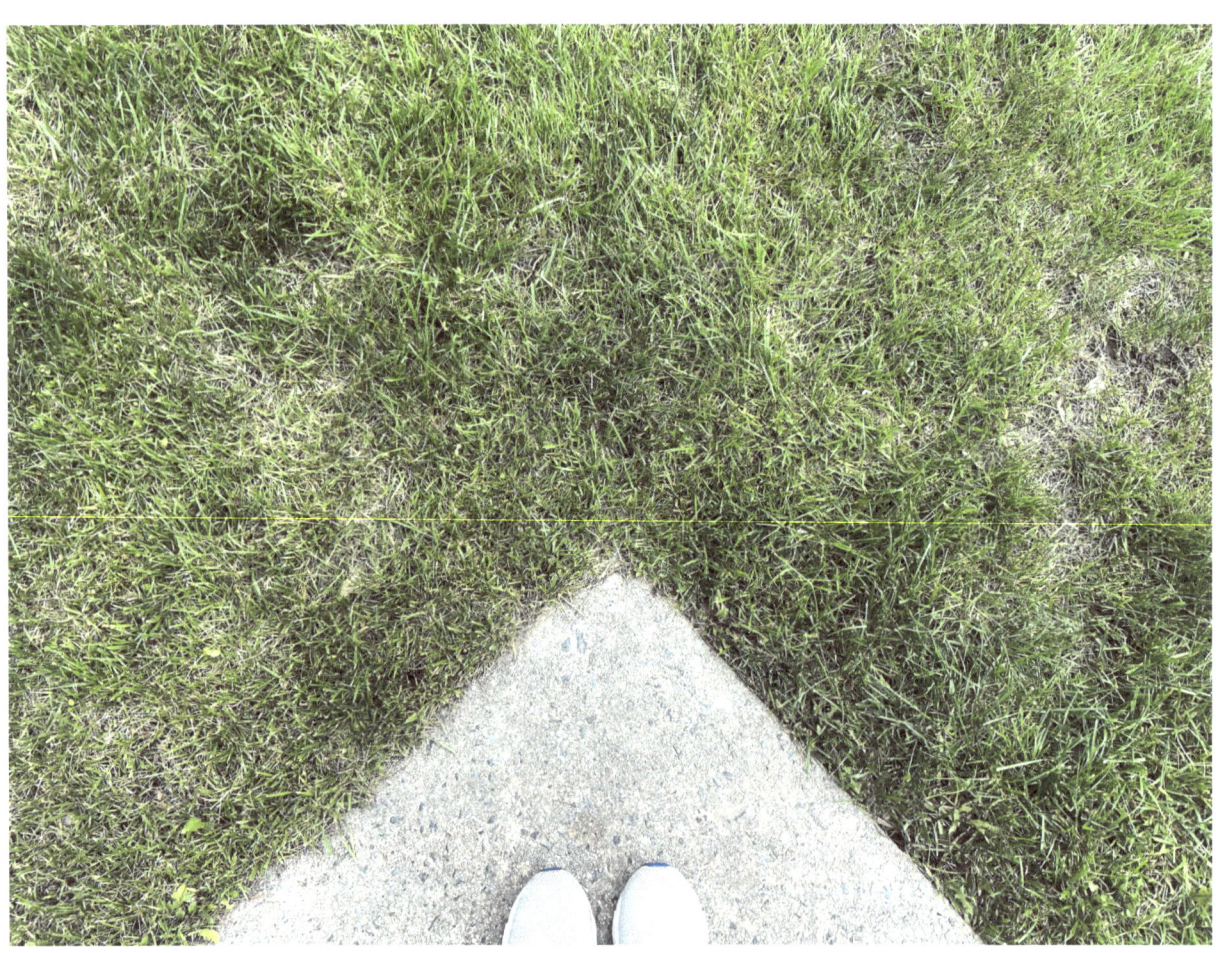

Landing #1, photography, 2021.

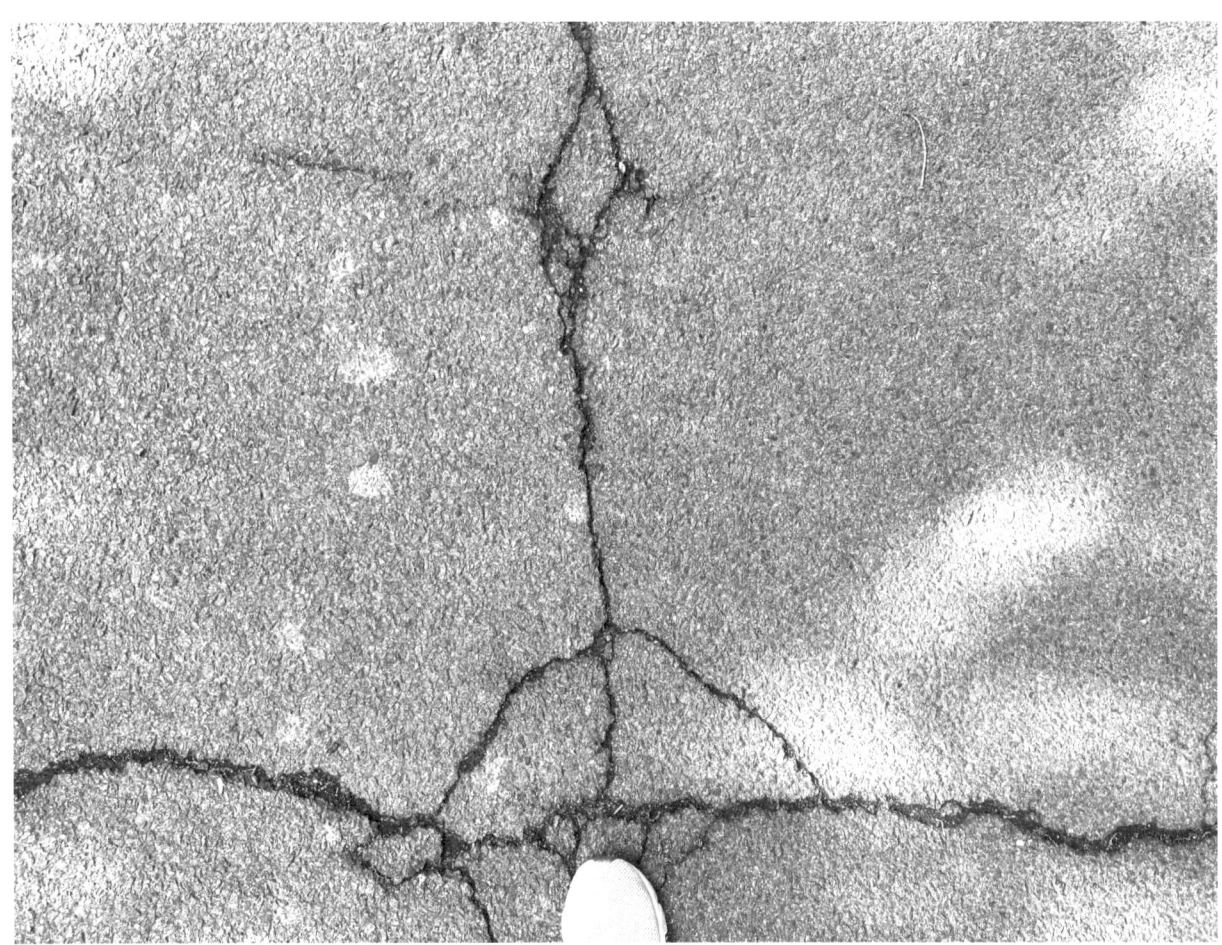

Landing #2, photography, 2021.

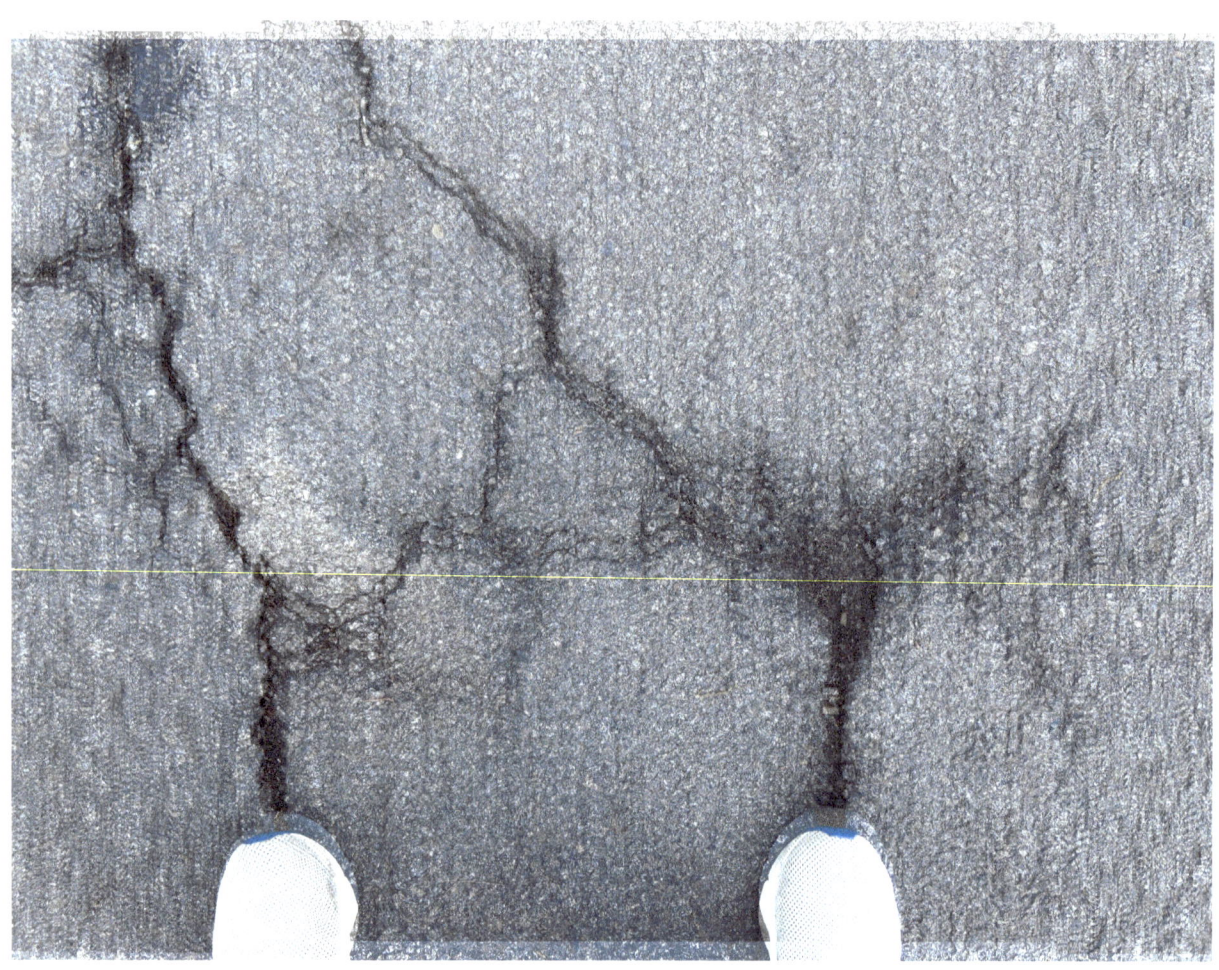

Landing #3, photography, 2021;

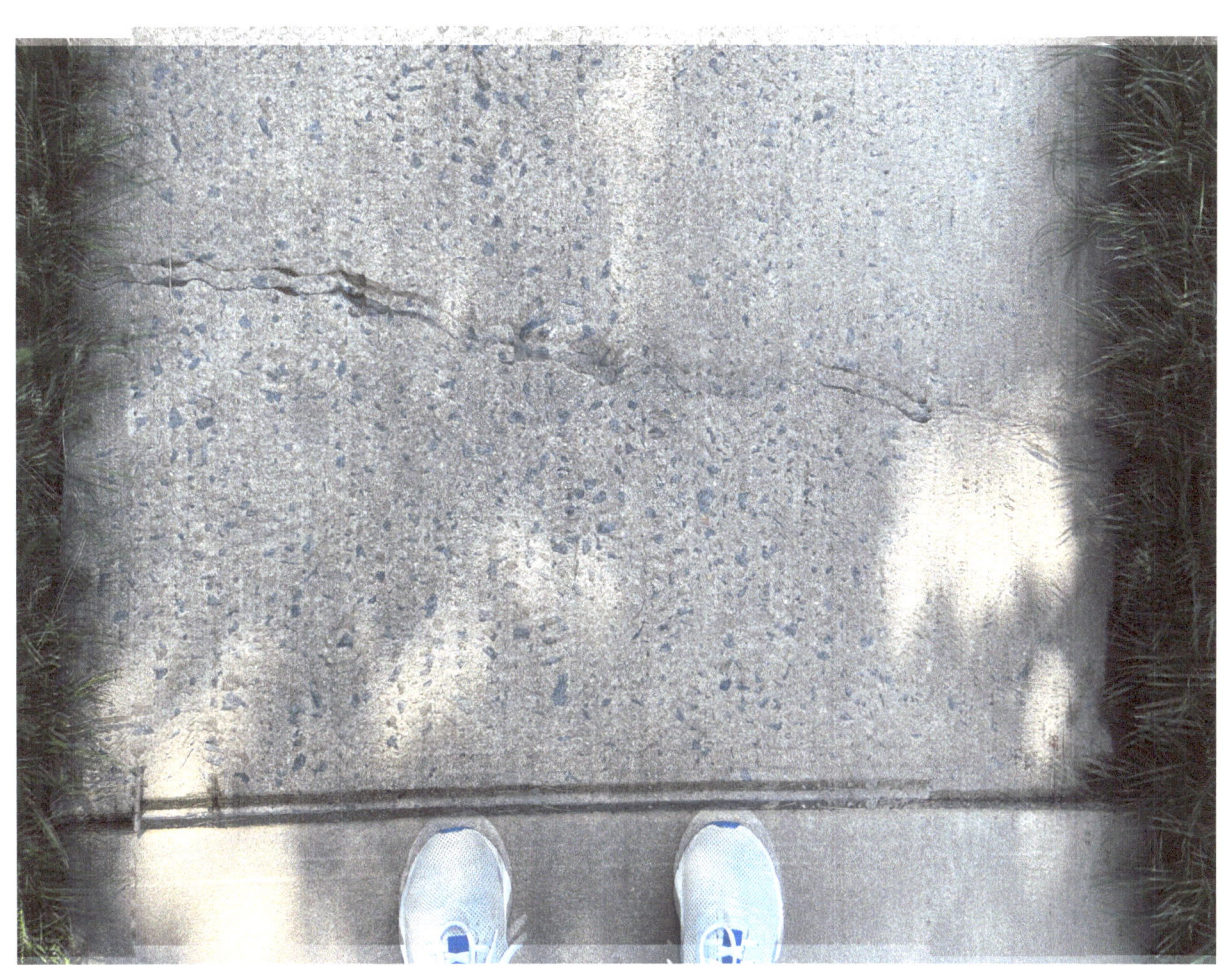

Landing #4, photography, 2021.

ZIQI MENG
Qingdao Laoshan District Maidao Middle School, China

- Bronze Award for Art, 5th Liberty Awards, International Society of Young Artists, USA, 2022.
- Level 10, Soft Pen Calligraphy, Shandong Student Art Test, China, 2022.
- Level 8, Soft Pen Calligraphy, Shandong Student Art Test, China, 2021.
- Gold Award for Art, 4th Liberty Awards, International Society of Young Artists, USA, 2021.
- Silver Award for Art, 3rd Liberty Awards, International Society of Young Artists, USA, 2020.
- Bronze Award for Art, 2nd Liberty Awards, International Society of Young Artists, USA, 2019.
- Rising Star Award, 1st Liberty Awards, International Society of Young Artists, USA, 2018.

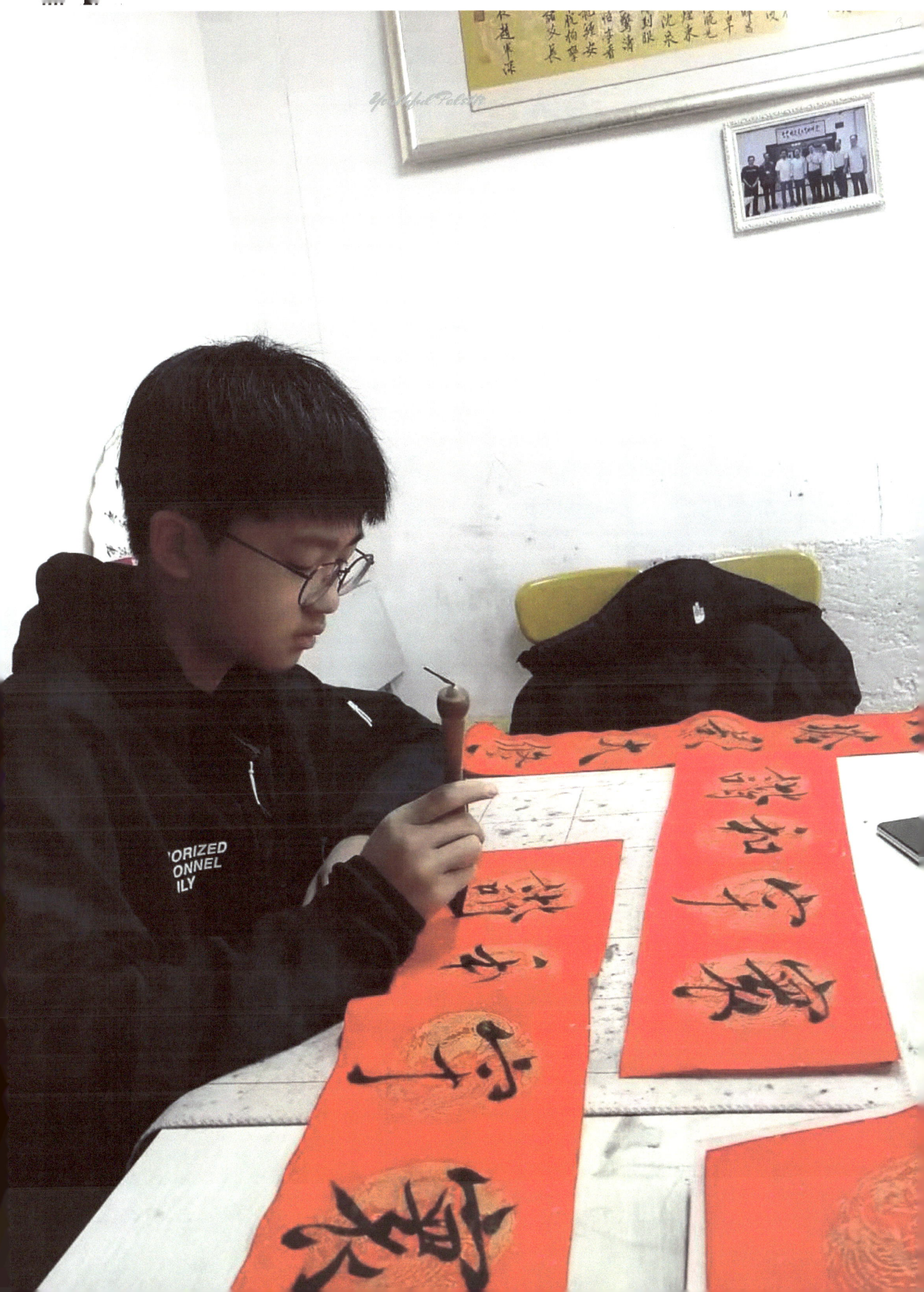

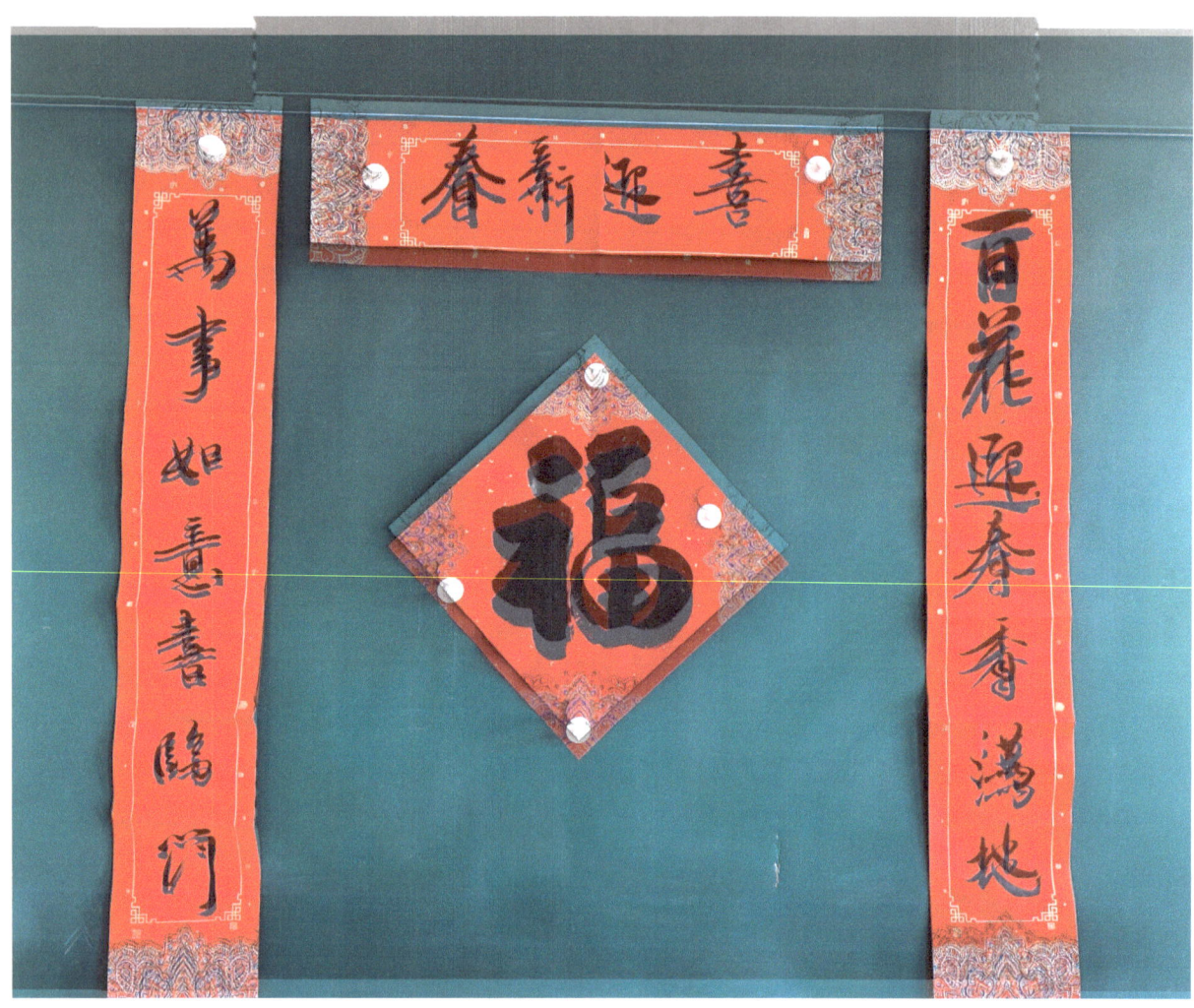

Happy New Year, calligraphy, 2022:

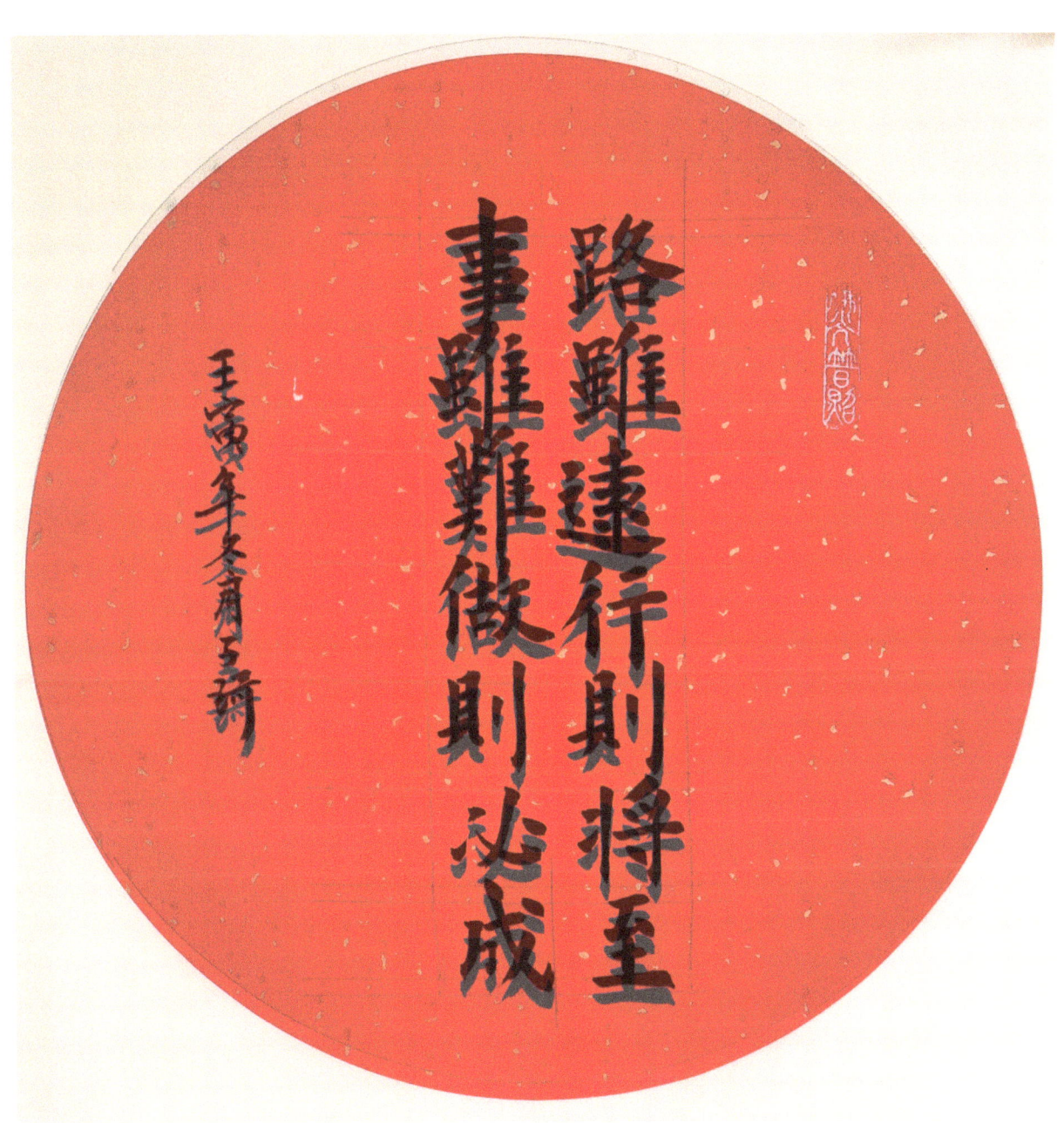

Although the Road Is Long, calligraphy, 2022.

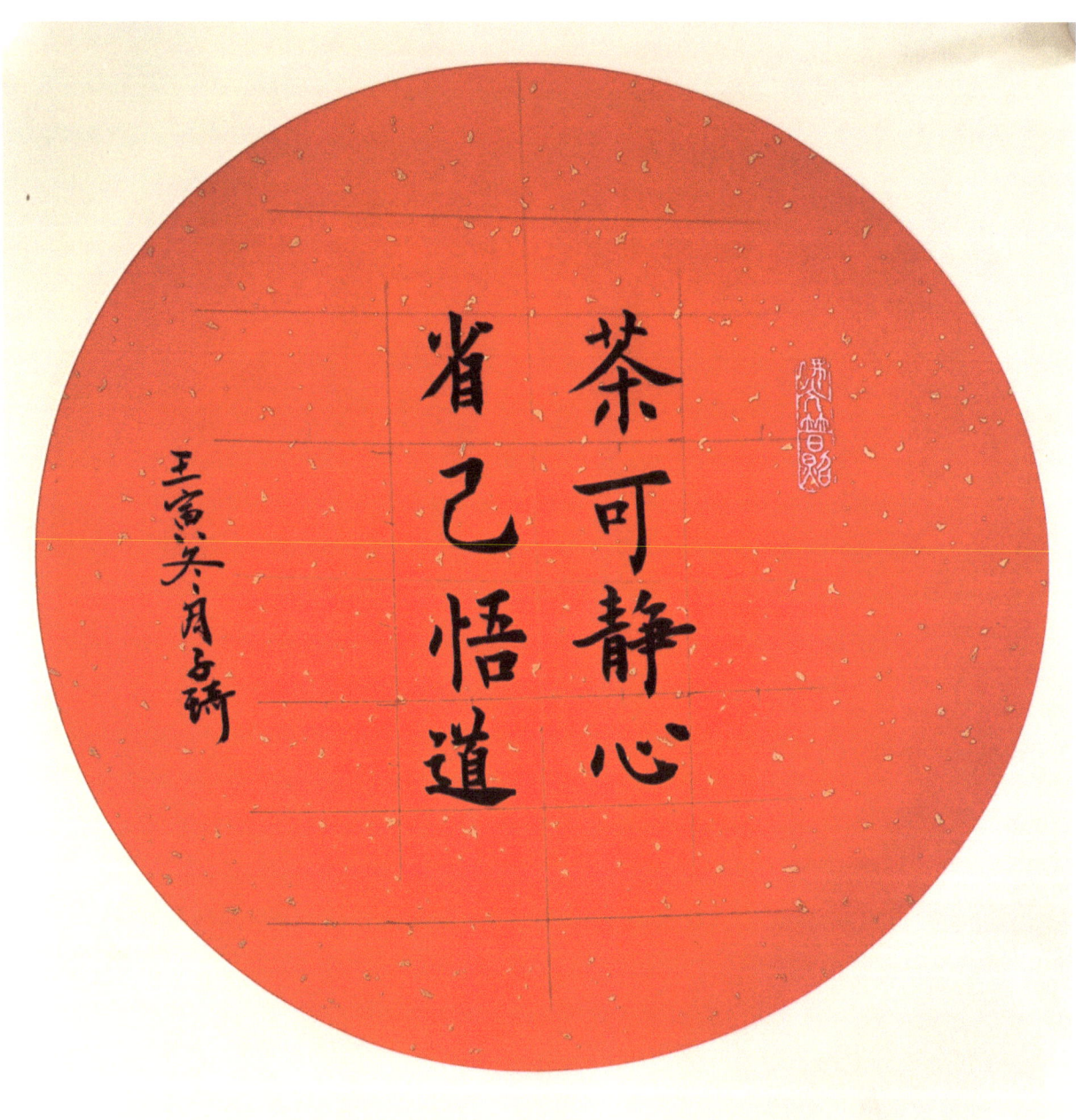

Enlightenment, calligraphy, 2022.

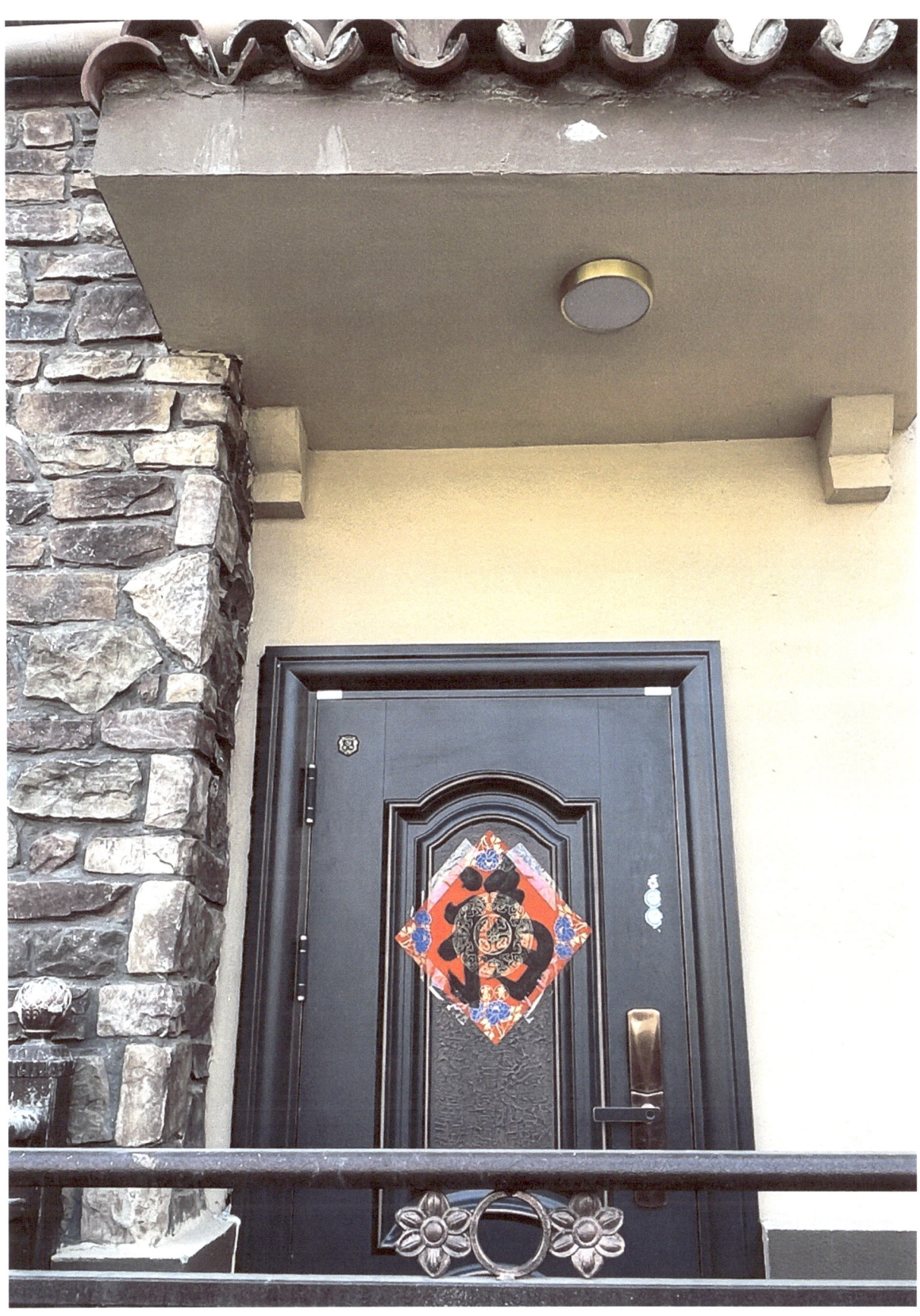

Blessing, calligraphy, 2022.

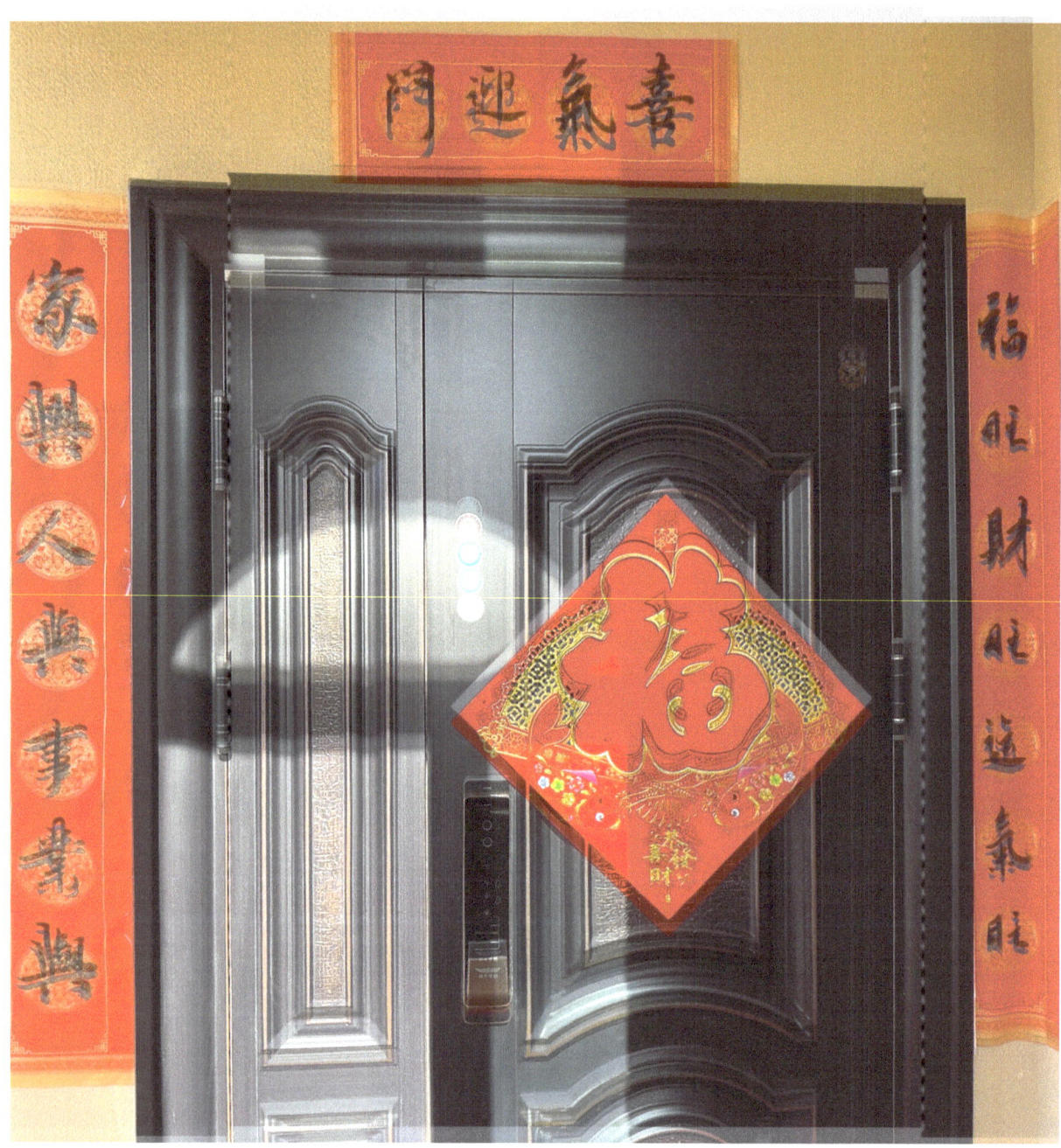

Good Luck Come To My Home, calligraphy, 2022.

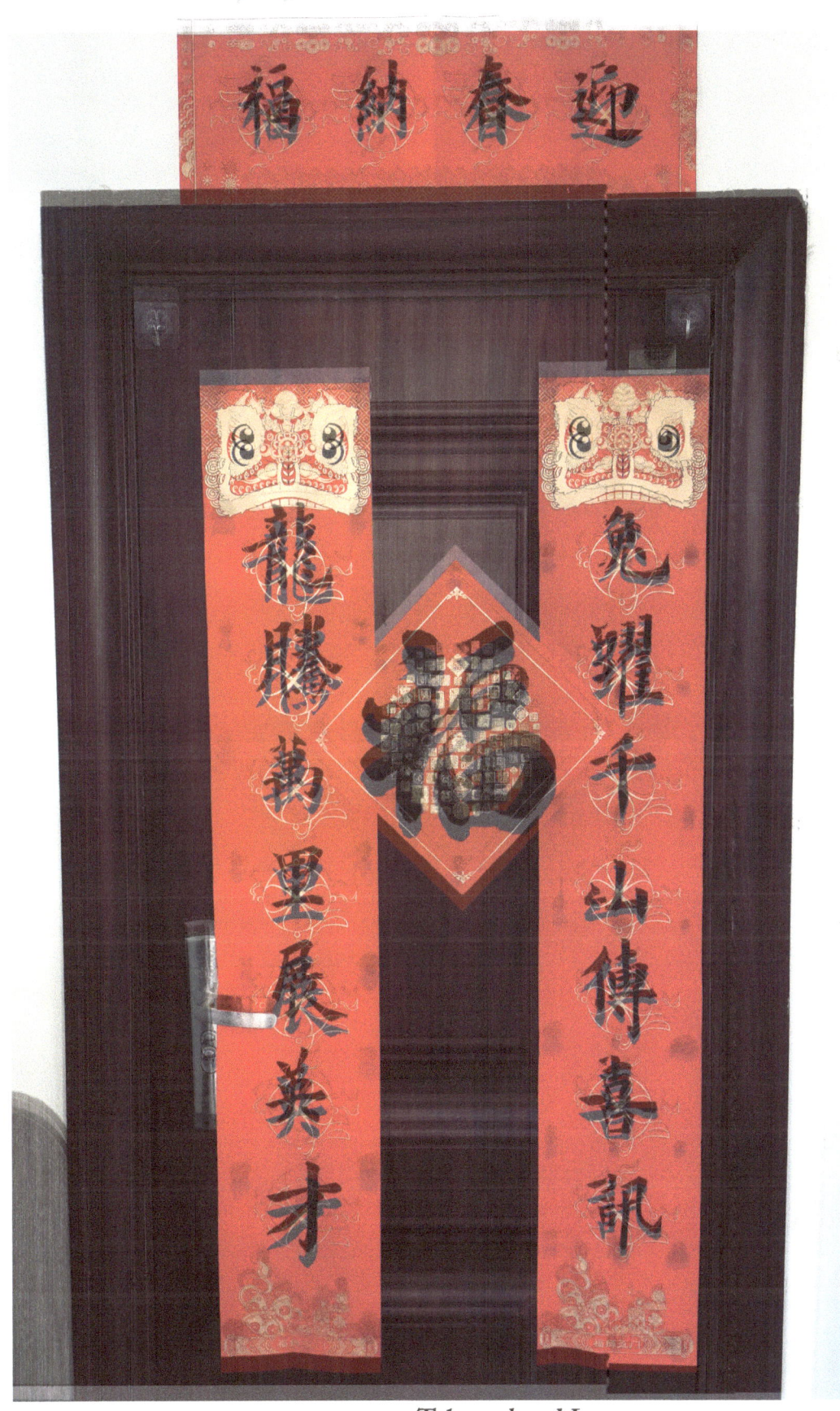

Talented and Lucky, calligraphy, 2022.

YIHAN HU
QINGDAO CHAOYIN ELEMENTARY SCHOOL, CHINA.

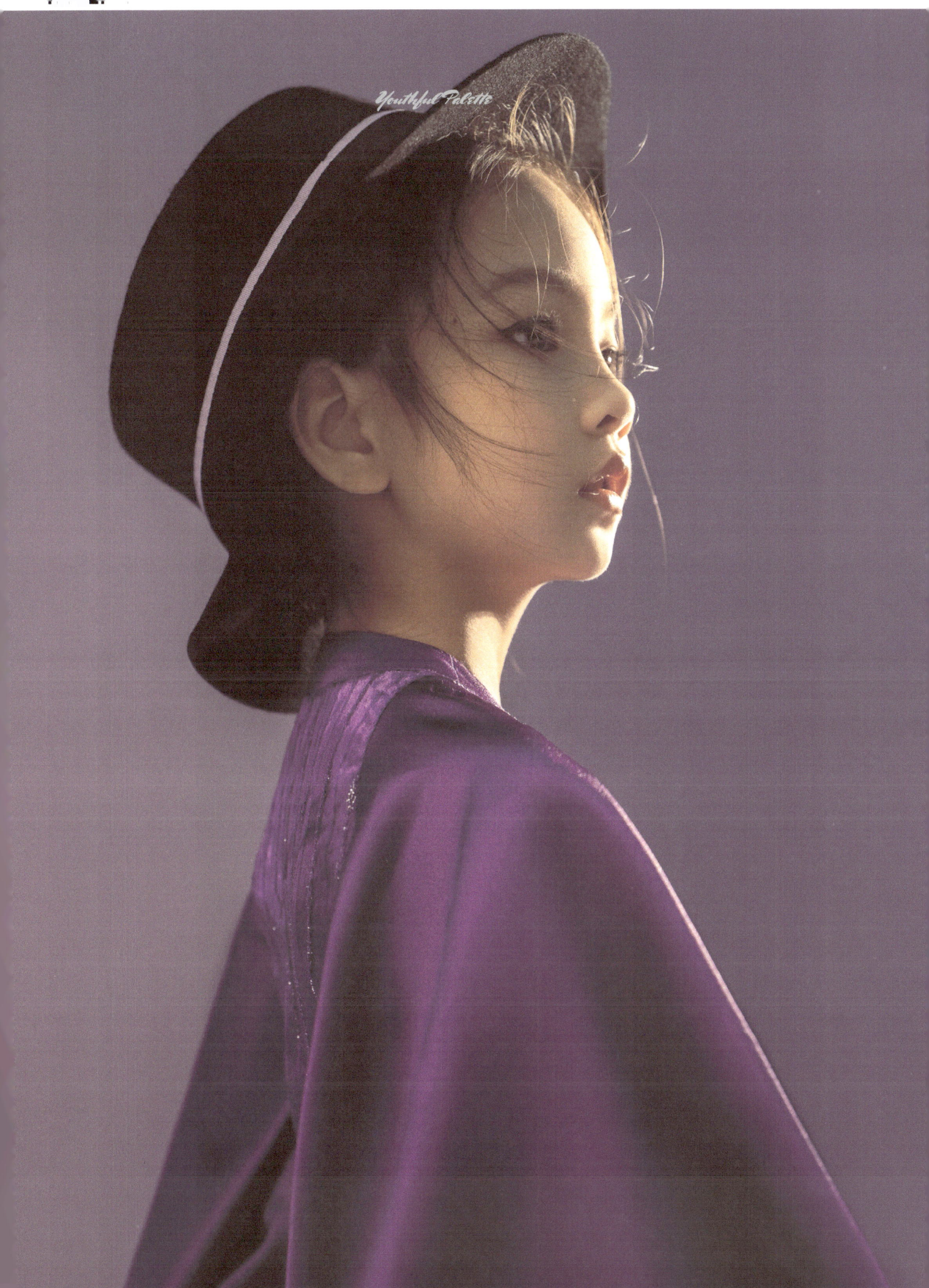

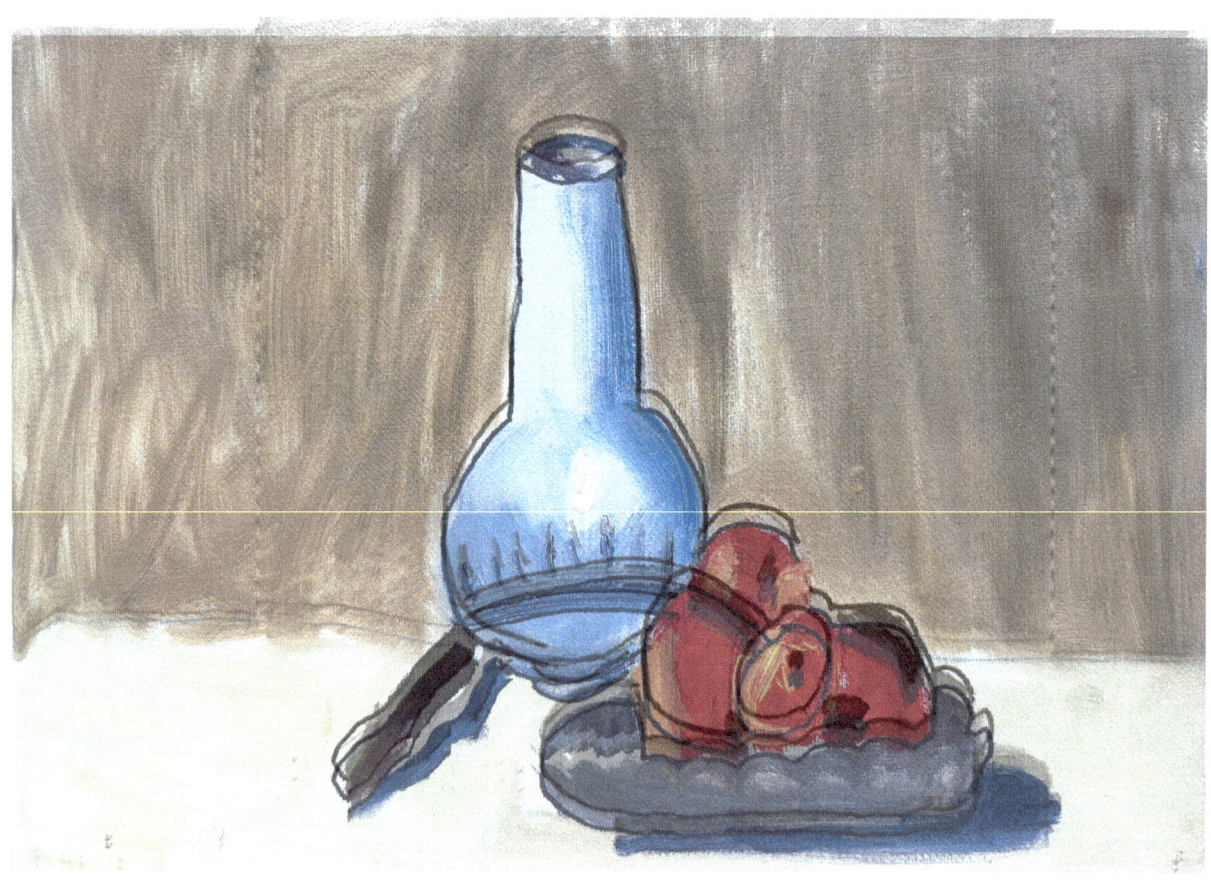

Learn to Paint a Vase and Fruit, oil on canvas, 2019.

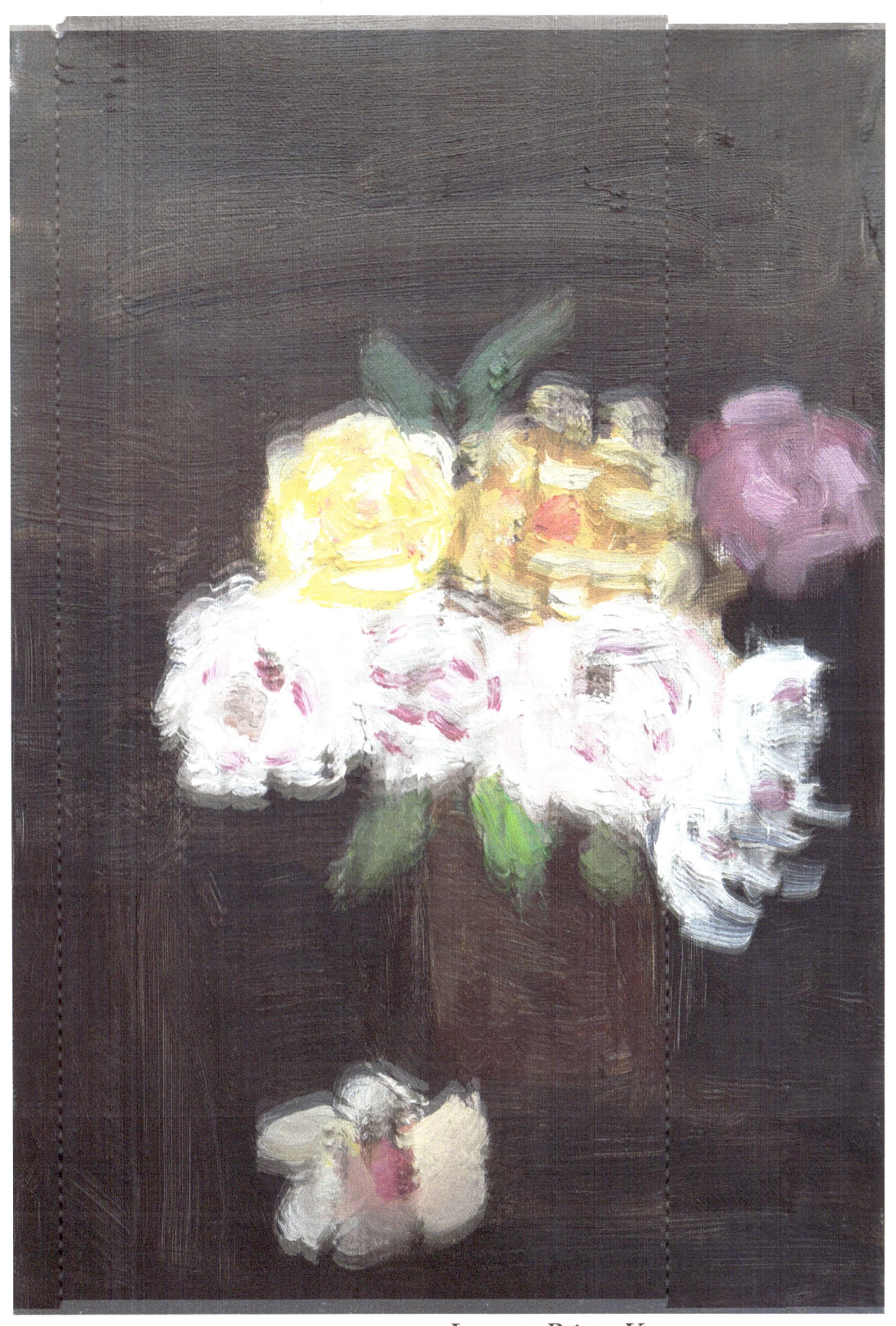

Learn to Paint a Vase, oil on canvas, 2019.

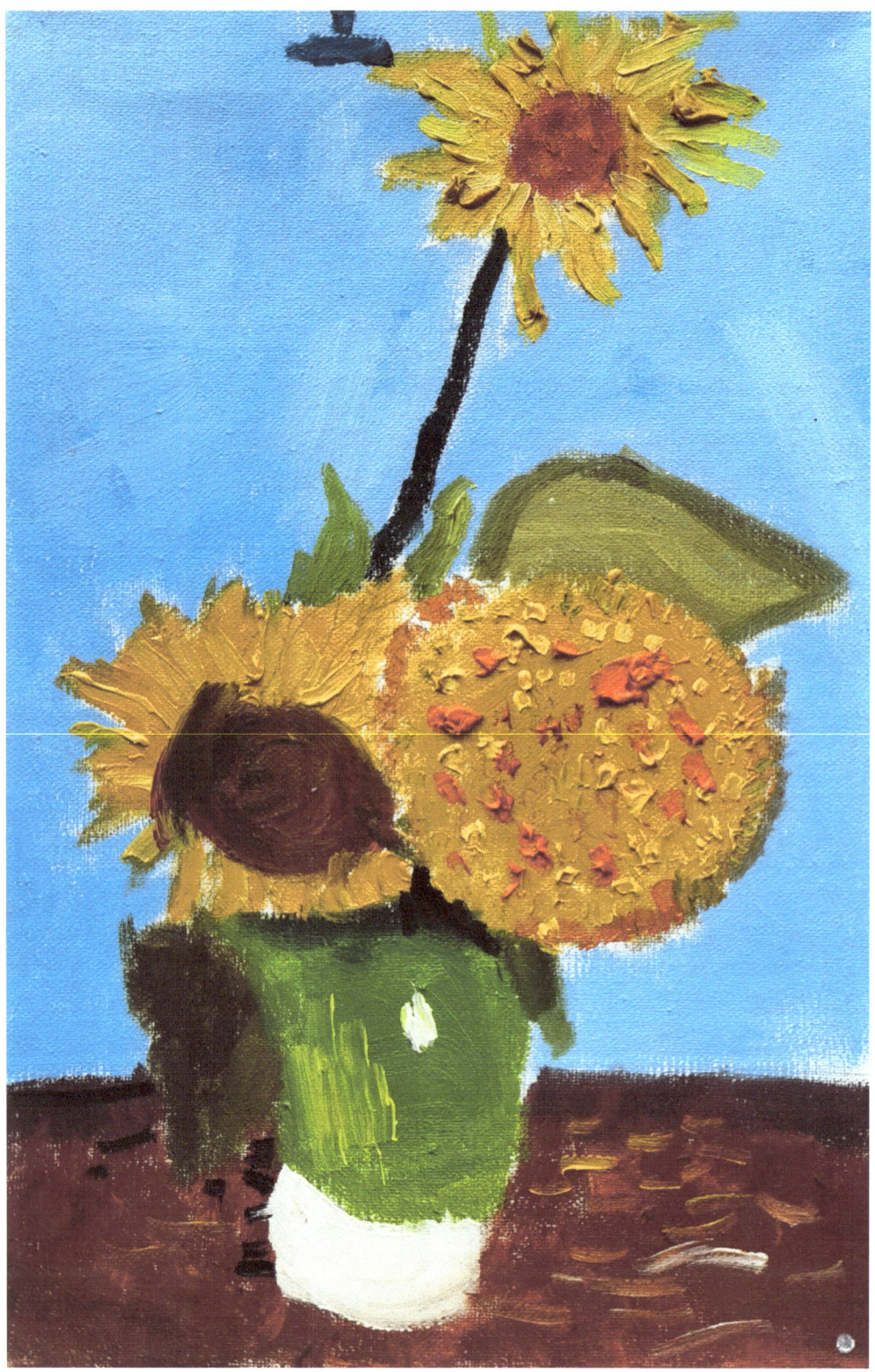

Learn to Paint Sunflowers like Van Gogh, oil on canvas, 2019.

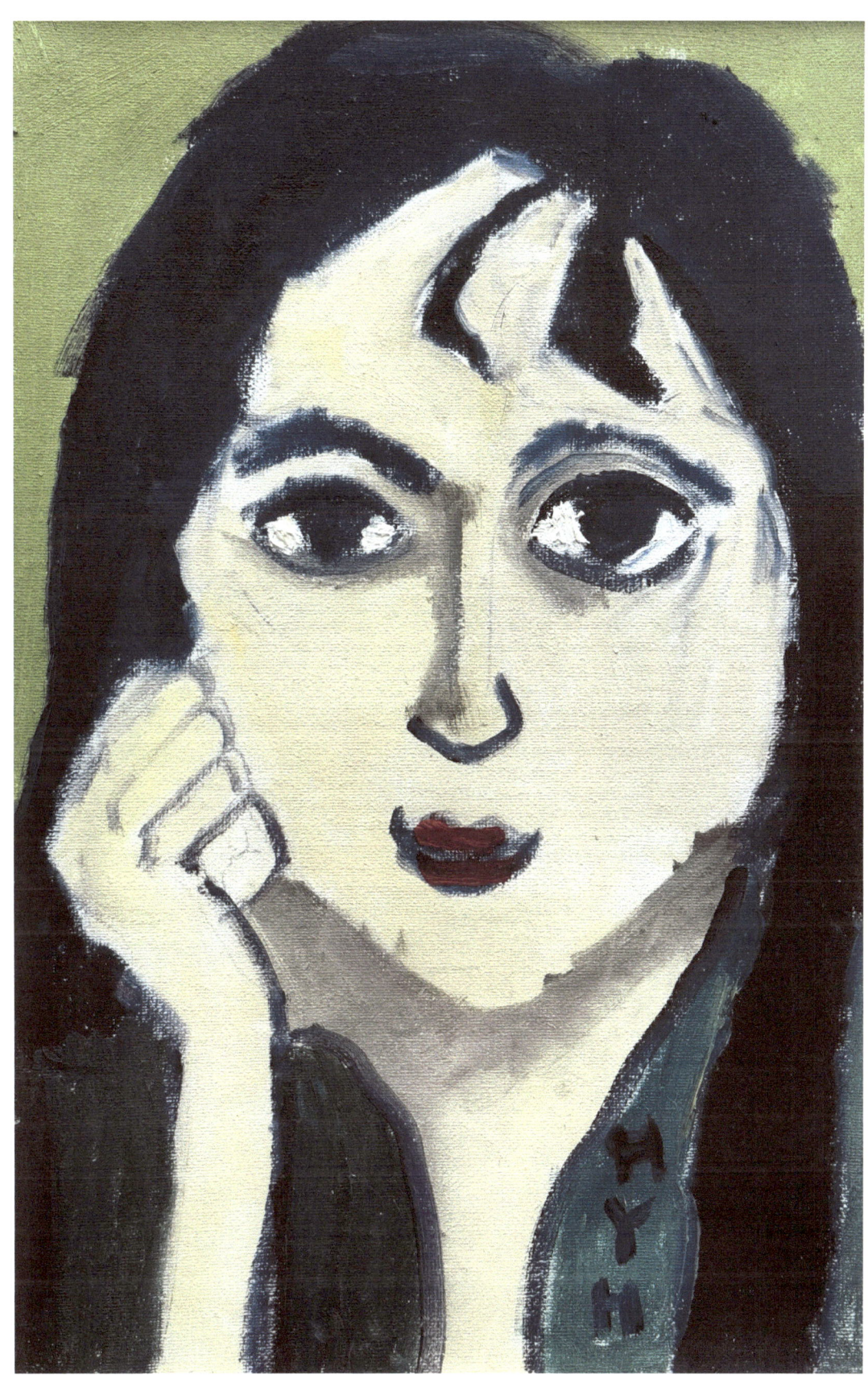

Learn to Paint a Lady like Matisse, oil on canvas, 2019.

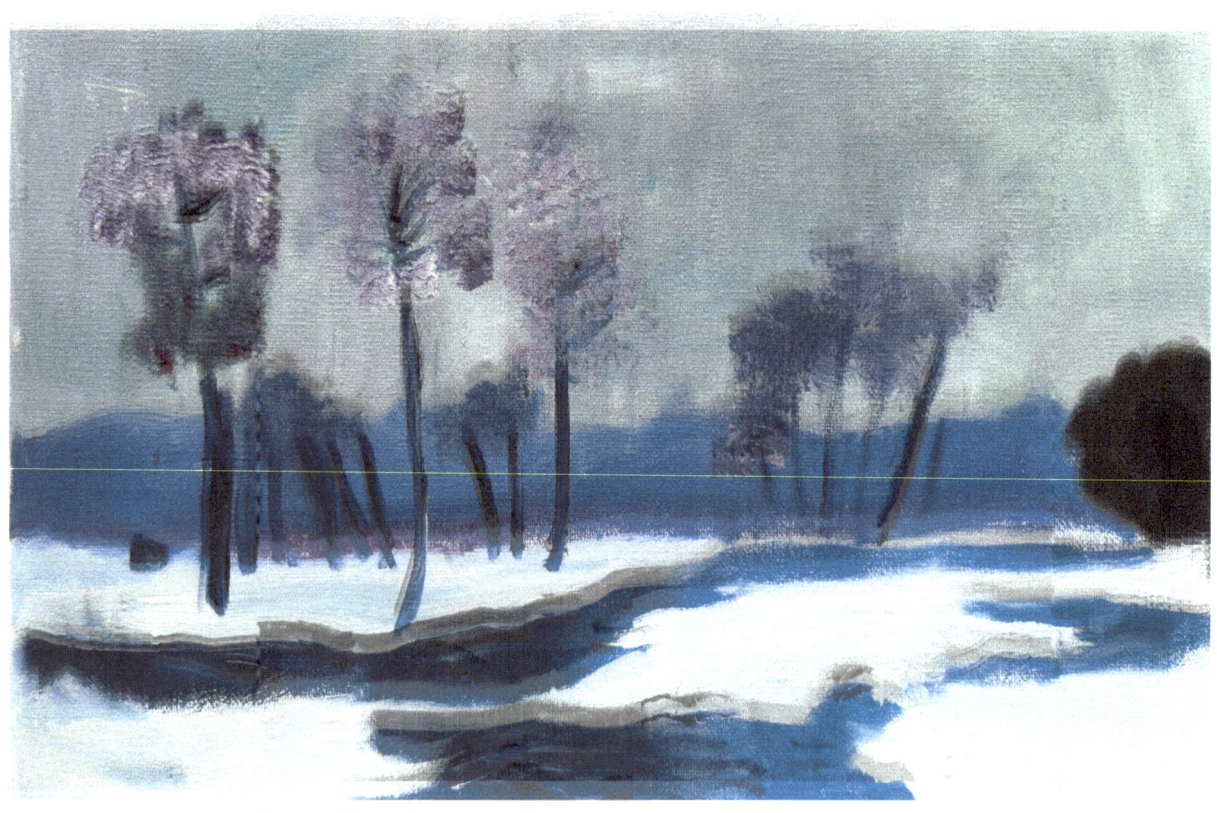

Learn to Paint a Grove Landscape, oil on canvas, 2019.

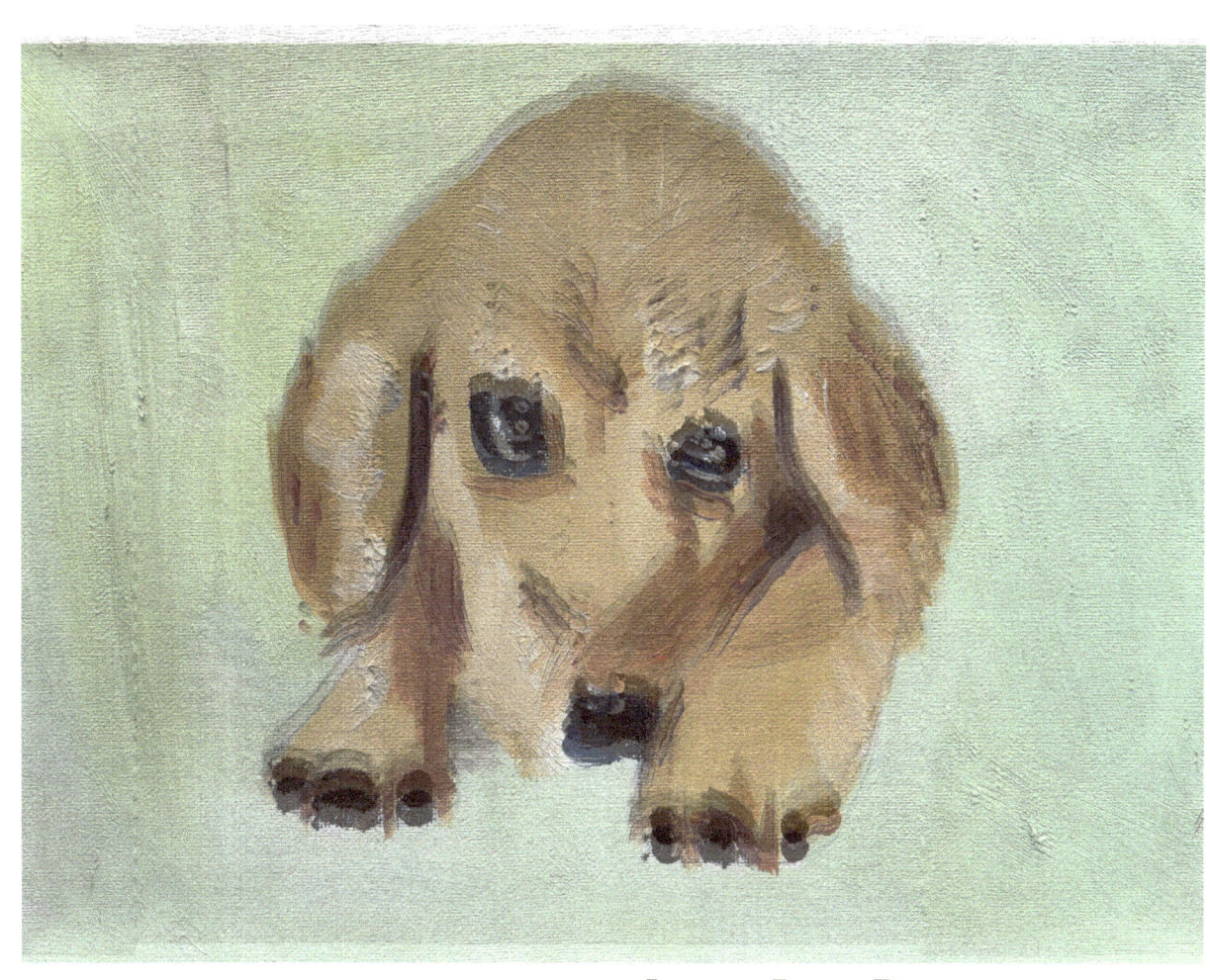

Learn to Paint a Dog, oil on canvas, 2019.

EMMA CHEN
COLLINGWOOD SCHOOL, CANADA.

- **Silver Award for Art, 5th Liberty Awards, International Society of Young Artists, USA, 2022.**
- **Excellence Award, Artopia Youth Society, Canada, 2022.**

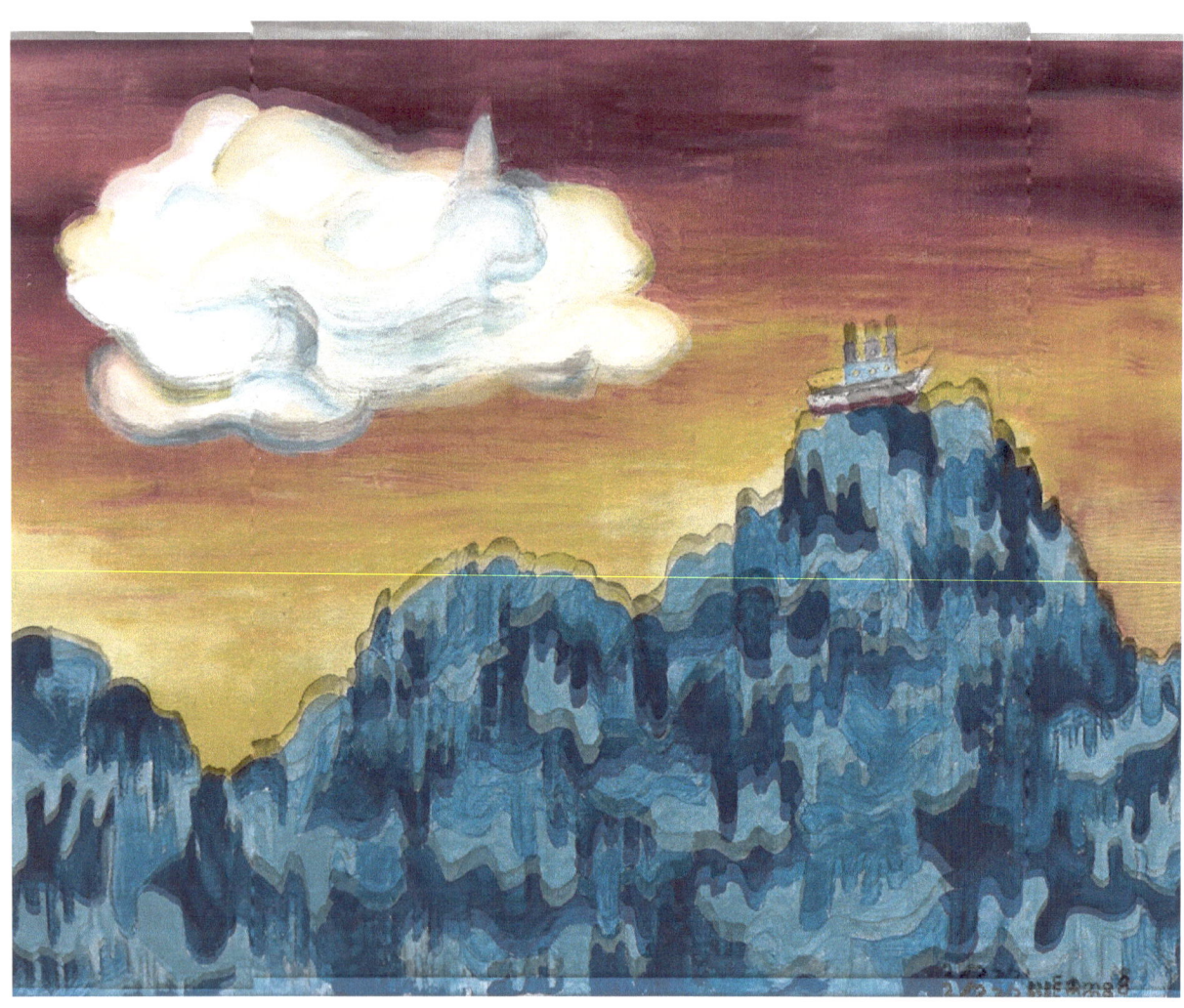

Time Story, acrylic on paper, 2020.

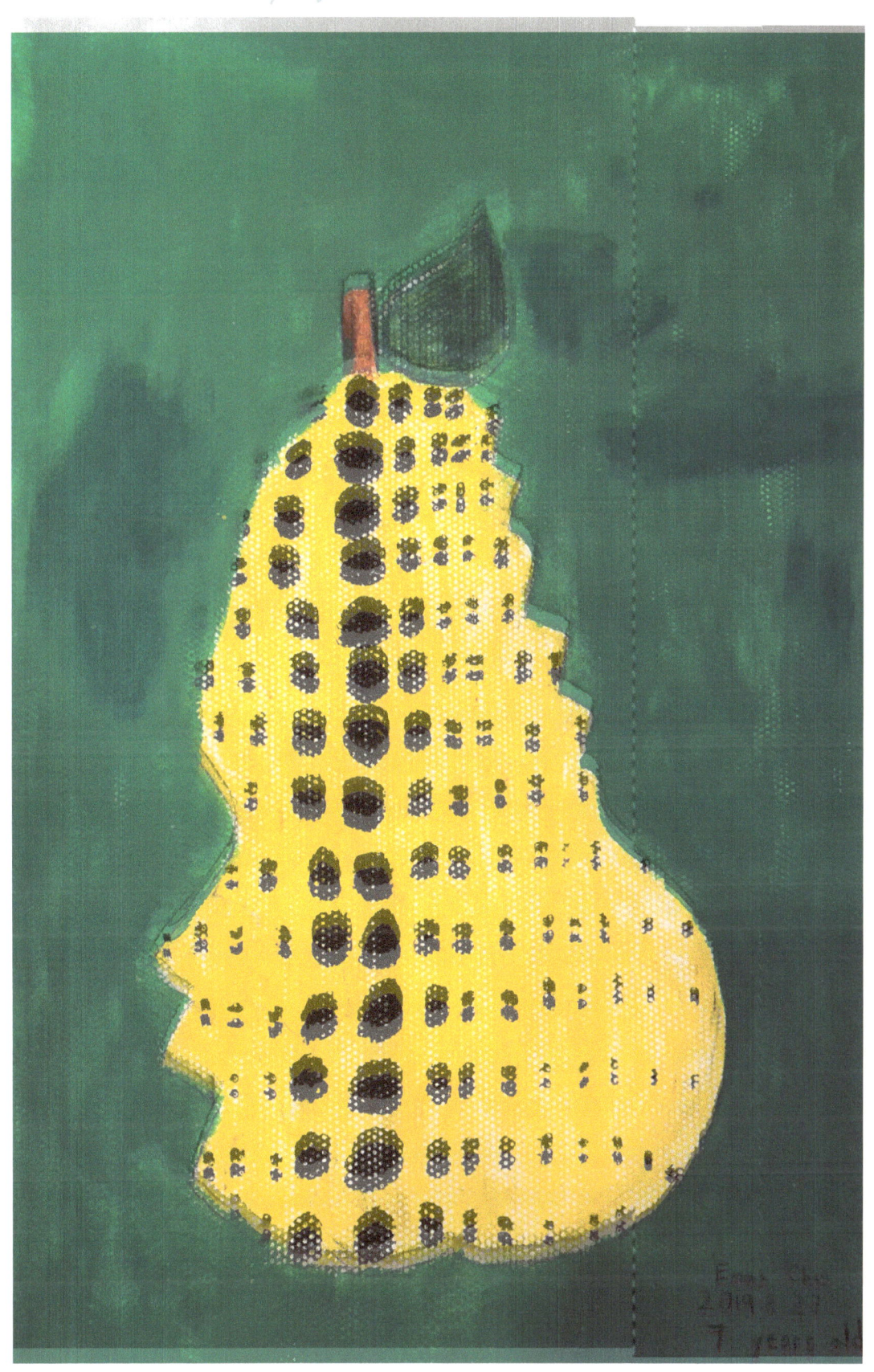

Pear, acrylic on paper, 2019.

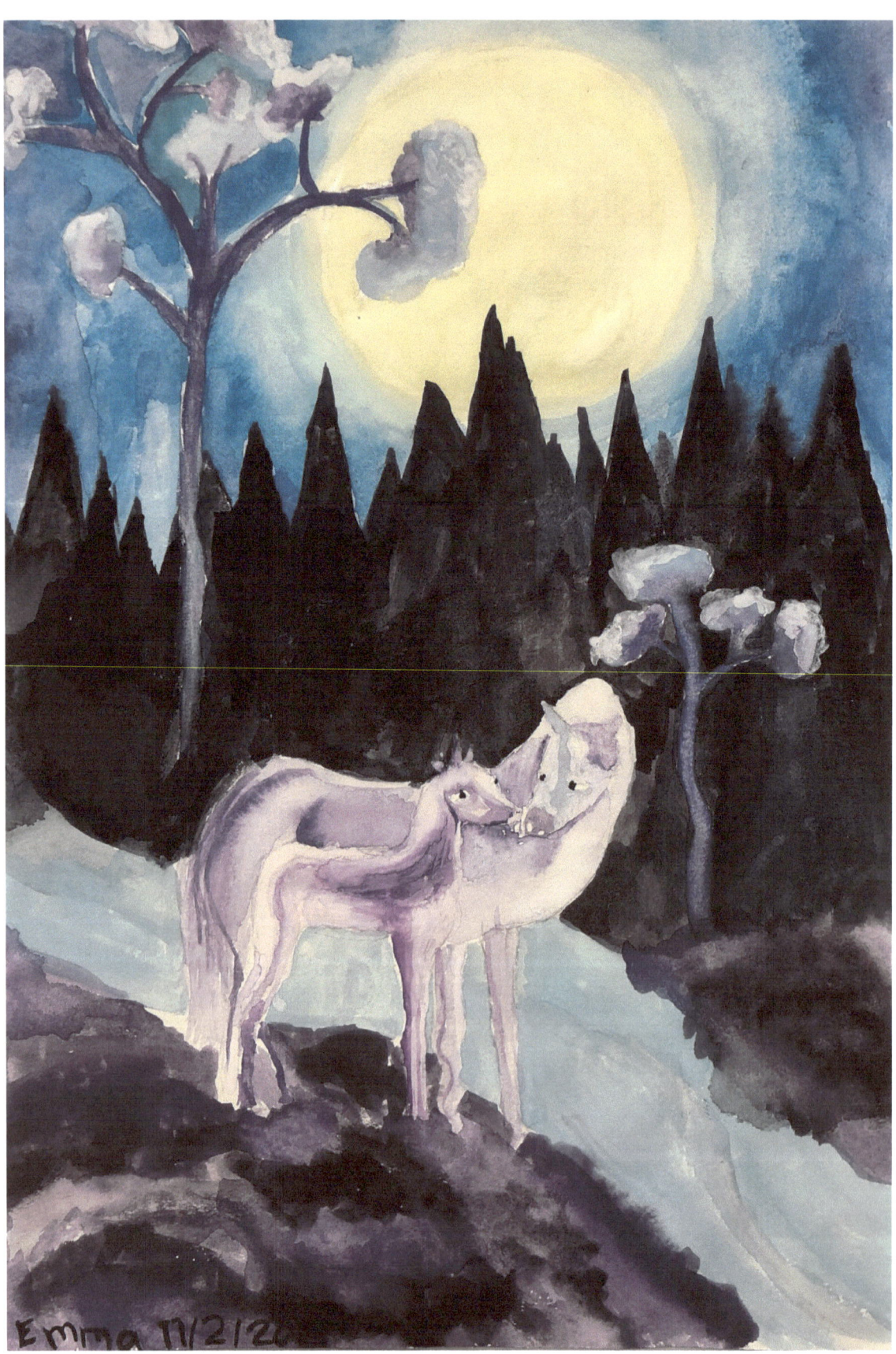

Mother and Daughter, gouache on paper, 2022.

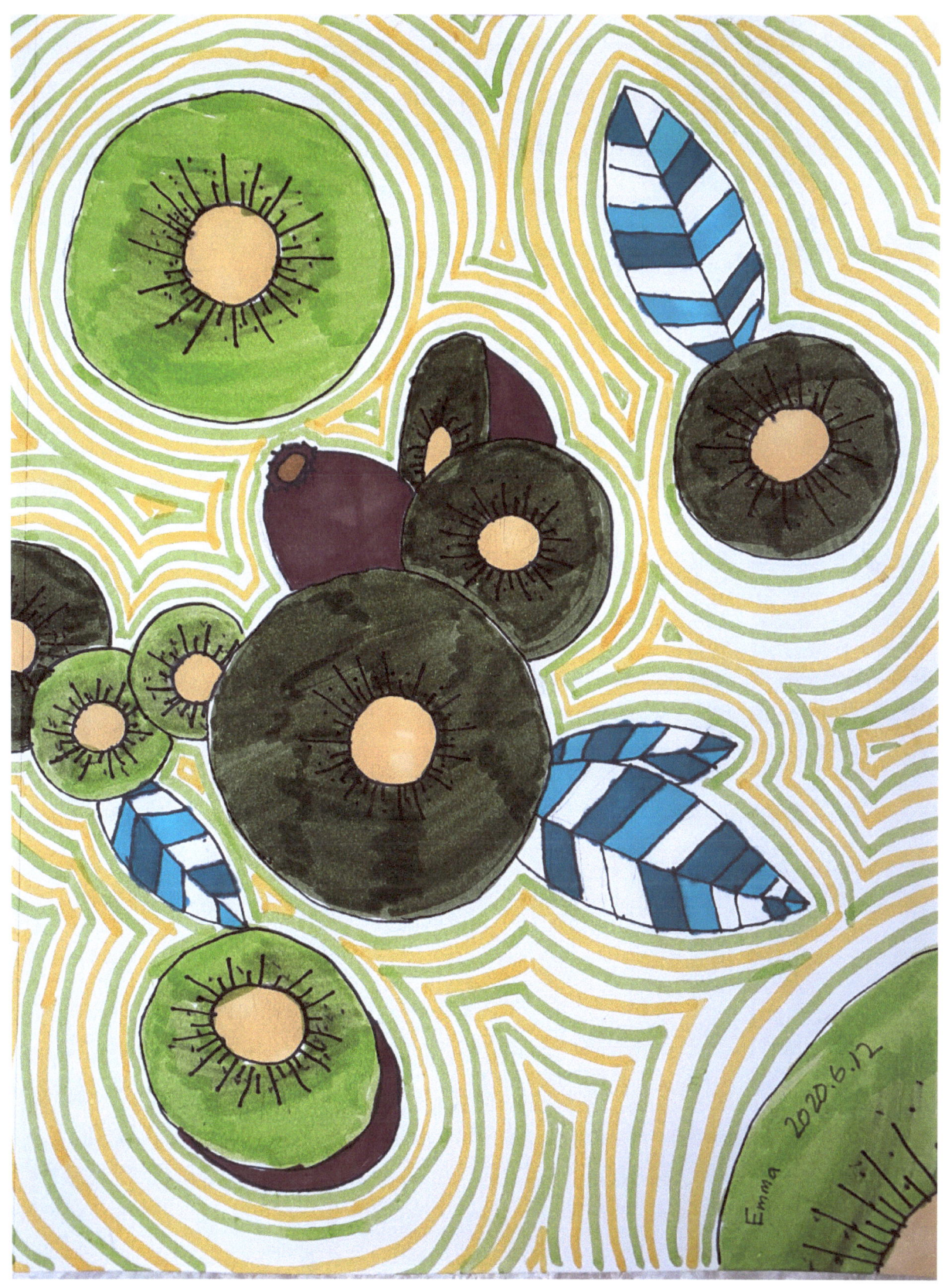

Scent of Flowers, paint pen on paper, 2020.

The "Vibrant Future" International Education Project for Young Artists Publications List

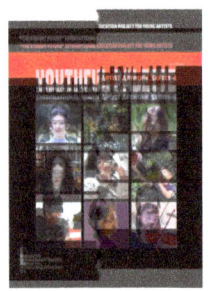

Youthful Palette: International Youth Artist Artwork Series-4, Los Angeles: Losget Press, 2023.

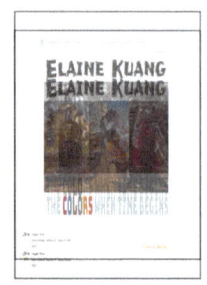

Elaine Kuang: The Colors When Time Begins, Los Angeles: Losget Press, 2022.

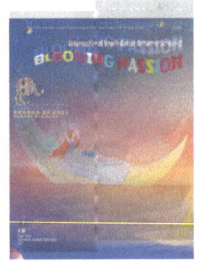

Blooming Passion: International Youth Artist Artwork Series-3, Los Angeles: Losget Press, 2022.

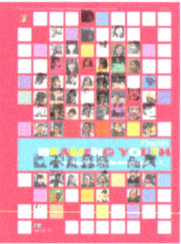

Beaming Youth: International Youth Artist Artwork Series-2, Los Angeles: Losget Press, 2021.

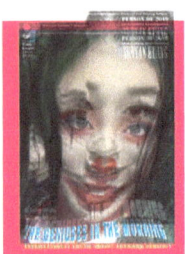

The Geniuses in the Morning: International Youth Artist Artwork Series-1, Los Angeles: Losget Press, 2020.

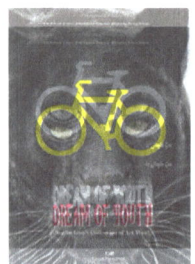

Dream of Youth, Los Angeles: Losget Press, 2019.

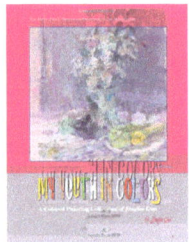

My Youth in Colors, Los Angeles: Losget Press, 2019.

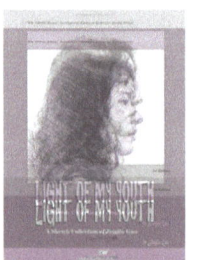

Light of My Youth. Losget Press, 2019.

The Young Picture Book Artists Program Publications List

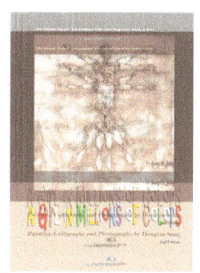

A Girl in Millions of Colors, Los Angeles: Losget Press, 2019.

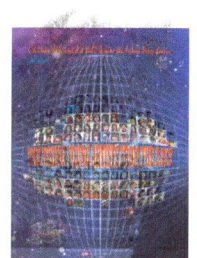

The Rising Young Artists from the East, Los Angeles: Losget Press, 2019.

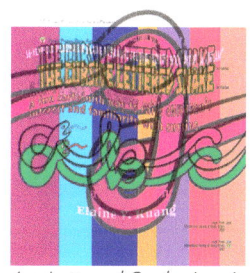

The Cursive Lettered Snake, Los Angeles: Losget Press, 2022.

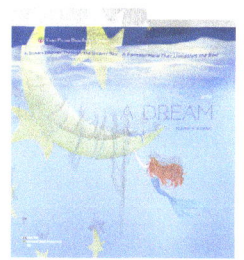

A Dream, Los Angeles: Losget Press, 2022.

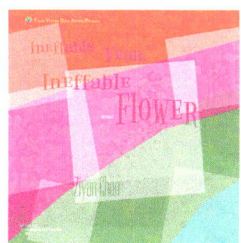

Ineffable Year, Ineffable Flower, Los Angeles: Losget Press, 2022.

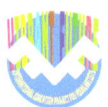

"Vibrant Future"
International Education
Project for Young Artists

Artists: Elaine V. Kuang, Jiajun Deng, Ziyan Chen, Rong Hong, Lujia Gao, Junkai Gong, Ziqi Meng, Yihan Hu, Emma Chen
Editor-in-Chief: Mark Harris
Editors: Jia Zhong, Elaine V. Kuang, Jiajun Deng
Cover designer: Jia Zhong, Elaine V. Kuang
Book designer: Jia Zhong, Jiajun Deng

 Copyright © 2023 by International Society of Young Artists
All rights reserved.

 Published in the United States by Losget Press, Los Angeles.
Originally published in paperback in the United States by Losget Press, in 2023.
Library of Congress Cataloging-in-Publication Data
Names: Kuang, Elaine V./ Deng, Jiajun/ Chen, Ziyan/ Gao, Lujia/ Gong, Junkai/ Meng, Ziqi/ Chen, Emma, authors.
Title: Youthful Palette: International Youth Artist Artwork Series-4/ Elaine V. Kuang, Jiajun Deng, Ziyan Chen, Lujia Gao, Junkai Gong, Ziqi Meng, Emma Chen.
Description: First edition. | Los Angeles: Losget Press, 2023.
Identifiers: LCCN: 2023902264/ ISBN: 978-1-951364-37-3
www.isoya.com
E-mail: isoya2018@gmail.com
First printing. 2023.